Goldberg Street

Goldberg Street

Short Plays and Monologues
by

David Mamet

Grove Press
New York

Published simultaneously in Canada
Printed in the United States of America

Library of Congress Cataloging-in-Publication Data

Mamet, David.
  Goldberg street.
  I. Title.
PS3563.A4345A6 1985 812'.54   84-73210
ISBN-10: 0-8021-5104-3 (pbk.)
ISBN-13: 978-0-8021-5104-9

Grove Press
841 Broadway
New York, NY 10003

07 08 09 10 15 14 13 12

Contents

INTRODUCTION: *Suitable for Framing*

Tradition has it that Shakespeare finished *King Lear* and handed it to Richard Burbage saying: "You son-of-a-gun, I've finally written one you can't perform."

I would like to say these pieces were done as experiments in form, rhythm, and sound; but in truth they were written as emotional meal tickets which would allow me to get through a day not consecrated to some major (longer) project and still think of myself as a writer.

The bad news is that I feel that some of these three- and ten-minute plays are the best writing I have ever done, and what in the world are they good for?

So I thank you for your interest in this collection.

I hope the pieces are fun to read and to perform—they were all fun to write.

David Mamet

Goldberg Street

Goldberg Street and *Cross Patch* were first presented live on WNUR Radio in Chicago on March 4, 1985, with the following cast directed by David Mamet:

Goldberg Street	*Cross Patch*
Mike Nussbaum	W. H. Macy
Susan Nussbaum	Mike Nussbaum
	Peter Riegert
	Colin Stinton

A man and his daughter talking.

Man: Goldberg Street. Because they didn't *have* it.

They had *Smith* Street—they had *Rybka* Street.

There was no Goldberg Street.

You can keep your distance and it's fine.

If a man is secluded then he feels superior. Or rage. But where's the good in that?

Daughter: There is no good in it.

Man: I'm not sure. And I'm not so sure. But sometimes... *(Pause.)*

And sometimes, also—you must stand up for yourself. Because it is uncertain... what we're doing here.

And masses of *people* do now this and now that; and *at the moment* you might say "this seems wrong," or "this seems attractive."

Popular delusions warp... you cannot say they are the product of one man.

Some men like hunting. I enjoy it myself.

Some men like to kill.

Many have killed. Many would say this is not a bad thing.

But they know it is.

Which is not to say they have not enjoyed it.

·   ·   ·   ·   ·

Man: A man would *wish*... *(Pause.)*

A man would wish someone to inform him...

I, if I man say, this is a good example—I am not mechanical but if something is broken and I *must* fix it there comes a point at which pride *in myself*—for the alternative is to say that I am not a man, or that I am an impotent or *stupid*... or, in some way unable to do those things many have done...

At one point I would say: "It now is mine to fix it."

When it's up to *me*—if there is no one there. . . then I *will* fix it—for it isn't hidden.

So with problems... those things where one *cannot* refer to someone.

At some point. One must say: *I* am the...

Daughter: ...the authority.

Man: ...the, *loneliness* that that entails, of course...and who would be so droll as to form a religion on ethical principles? (*Pause.*)
  And one is alone.
  And *so* one is...
  And so what.
  From *that* one may say "well, then I can proceed..."
  Lost in the wood you must say "I am lost."

Daughter: You killed the deer.

Man: The man in *Bregny*...(*Pause.*)
  Men hunted them with automatic weapons.
  Which is not a sporting way and it is not an effective way.
  Because you can't *aim* them, truly...

Daughter: ...because they jump.

Man: They *do* jump. And...you can aim the first shot, of course....
  But we were taught to fire them from the hip. Held on the sling to give it tension.
  And they *hunted* them, and, as you couldn't aim your shot, the animal, hit badly...
  Ran.
  Died.
  Left a blood trail, but they couldn't follow it.
  Or wouldn't.
  Although they were country boys.
  And, I'm sure...revered life.
  Loved hunting...
  ...anyway

(*Pause.*)

  They couldn't read a compass.
  In Arkansas one time we were lost. The leader asked if anyone could read a compass. We'd all heard the lecture. I said, well, I'd never *held* one, but I heard it, I supposed I ...took it. Read it. Followed the map.

Led us back to camp. It was easy enough. None of it was difficult.

And they put me in for the Unit. When they asked for volunteers.

Which may have been a joke. It was a joke. For anti-Semitism in the army. Then. Even now... (*Pause.*)

Even for, and especially then which I see as...

If you look at the world you have to laugh. They scorned me, as I assume they did, for those skills they desired to possess. And it was funny I had them.

To them. Lost in the woods. It seems simple enough. If you just take away the thought someone's coming to help you. (*Pause.*)

Daughter: You never see them?

Man: No, although we were close. In a way. Over there. Where would we...

I have no desire to go down south. (*Pause.*) To go visiting at all.

Daughter: You went to France.

Man: I did. It was the Anniversary. I wanted to see.

Daughter: What did you see? (*Pause.*)

Man: People. (*Pause.*) I saw the town.

Daughter: Had it changed?

Man: No. It hadn't changed. Just as the world has changed. (*Pause.*)

Daughter: I heard they saw you.

Man: Yes. They saw me. There's always someone there.

Laying flowers—it's right by the cliff. I mean the cliff is right beside the road. They... (*Pause.*)

Daughter: They knew you.

Man: I was... no, they didn't know me. They saw someone standing... (*Pause.*)

A man spoke English. He went in the pub. He must have said, he said something like "one of them's come back." And, in the cemetery... they came over there.

Daughter: You were reading the stones?

Man: They're crosses, really... (*Pause.*) Yes. I was looking for the names.

Daughter: Did you find them?

Man: I thought that I would not remember them. I... but I ... (*Pause.*)

People from the pub came out. (*Pause.*) They said, "You were here."

Yes. We wept.

Patton slapped that Jewish boy.

They said... (*Pause.*)

Daughter: They remembered you. (*Pause.*) They remembered what you'd done.

Man: They sent me for a joke. Because I read the compass. I was glad to go. I knew they thought me ludicrous. Our shame is that we feel they're right. (*Pause.*) I... have no desire to go to Israel. (*Pause.*) But I went to France.

Cross Patch

Cross Patch
Draw the latch
Sit by the fire and spin.

Mother Goose

Scene: *A meeting hall.*

Characters: *Speakers on the dais, members of the audience.*

Master of Ceremonies:...and of the European Section?

Assistant:...ten.

M.C.:...and of the Home Section?

Assistant: Two.

M.C.: Two of the Home?

Assistant: Yes.

M.C.: Two. Yes. Aaaaaaand...Thank you. (*He addresses the hall.*)

Our Friends. Of the Green Division. Thank you. I would like to introduce Doctor William J. Pierce, who is known to you.

A...who needs no introduction, but I will avail myself of the honor of giving him one. First in the hearts of all those who deeply love freedom—first in the fearful estimation of those who *oppose* it. You have seen him on this stage, and you have seen him in the Nation's Press. And in its consciousness. As he...throughout the Years since the Second...a veteran of three wars; holding the reserve, as you know, he...prefers to be addressed by his medical title ...the reserve rank of Brigadier General in the Armed Forces of the United States. May we meditate on that for a brief instant, as he has said, from his, as I am sure you have read, *Cross Patch—The View of a Free Man*, by William J. Pierce; which is, as he has said, why he prefers to present his public face as a *citizen*, rather than a soldier. A great soldier, who wrote: "Armed: what better word to signify...a sense of pride, a sense of Honor, of our Sacred Charge—if we look to the Knights of Old, what did it signify? That one was *pledged to stand*—that, in assuming arms—we pledge ourselves accountable for our *acts*, for our *beliefs*, and *to* all those in our charge...to *stand*...'til *death*...at our posts...."

"And what source of pride," he writes, "...it gave to me...in our posts through the years...numbering thirty years...to say, to paraphrase, to reverse that lovely phrase written to the Corinthians, to say: 'what I am with you frightens me, what I am *for* you comforts me.'" My friends: William J. Pierce.

• 9

The audience applauds. William J. Pierce *moves to the podium.*

Pierce: Mr. Chairman. My friends. What must a man feel who has won the lottery?

In papers every day.

You see a man...a *working man.* Who's been awarded. Some gigantic sum. Millions of...This man's life is changed. To his wife, to his friends he says: "I'm as I was before— the things which gave me pleasure still will do. Those things I cherish will not be affected by this great fortune...."

To himself he says, "How will I change? *Surely* this sign from God"—how can he see it otherwise? Singled from millions of men, his hope *alone* blest—surely he must, in his heart, see it as a proof of divine providence, of endorsement of that secret thought (we all have had it) "I am *blessed.* I am a special man."

Let's stop a moment here.

On one extreme you see this thought expressed in Messianic Dreams, dreams of the demagogue—illusions of grandeur...

And on the bottom of the scale we see those (and we see them every day) oppressed, downtrodden, *devoid* of the most minimal modicum of Self-Esteem—slunk in the gutters, in the alleyways. Cowering in jobs they despise, weak, subservient, subserviated to their inability to *avow* their desires—to be Special. To be blest. To be *singled out for the good each of us knows is in his breast.*

And so we have two aberrations of the norm: Delusions of Grandeur, and, on the other hand, a suicidal wish to be ignored, to be punished, for—finally—for harboring that same wish for a Divine Love.

The ordinary man—like ourselves, let us say,...one day content, the next day not; in some things talented, in some things dull; full of pride, full of hidden fears, feelings of... *Torn Every Day* between that part of him which says "There is a god—be humble, find a meaning in this life," and "Go your way, get those things which can give you comfort, think of nothing, simply live and die."

This man, like you and me, when his most hidden wish

is broadcast to the world, what does he do? When, yes, the heavy hand of Providence taps him and says, "You are the one—among all—those who have watched and prayed—you are..." and frees the man from want. And from material anxiety, and sets him...*as* a City on a Hill—to those in whose midst he happily toiled, and in whose happy midst he never will again.... This man...abstracted from his home, translated to a pinnacle, assaulted by *greed...fear...greed ...hatred...not* unlike the Christ, for was it his goodness they hated? *All* of them were good. They killed him for that he had been preferred...as that man who had won a contest and had wished to win. My parallel...(*Pause.*)

My friends. In this world. As molecules move, as pigeons on the lawn move, as the stars in *their* predestined sway...so in the affairs of our so imperfect striving breed, so we are governed by forces we cannot see. Nor *ever* understand. Endorsed by Providence—why? What *course* shall we take? Our holy land? To, messianically proclaim, "Yes. Yes. I am the...you have waited for the one!" Or, as the abject wretch, say, "Forget me, I will not hear the call."

Our happy land.

What course shall we...

Blest by a Jealous God, or blest by Random Chance with Freedom. How shall we enjoy it?

Freed from Fears...

Single out, yes. We must acknowledge it...our lives *have* changed.

The Signal of the World—that shining city...we can never shrink out of the world's gaze, or quiet that gaze through force.

Where can we find humility? (*Pause.*)

The force of arms. An armed man, blest by God, with the strength of *will*...

That is, with...*not* blind to the essence of this life, which is, that it is fleeting. With the will to say: "Not as a gambler, rather as a *priest* I consecrate those things..."

Listen to me:...not, not to my *possession*...given to my *charge*...as *steward* of this life...of those great gifts, of the eternal gift of freedom...

I will *guard* that trust, as of another whom I love... *sans* bravery or show, or the desire of praise, but through my understanding of my place. Under God. With my fellow men.

My blessing is a charge and my arms are a sign: (the bearing of arms) that I do *accept* that charge... as did the Knights of Old... I find that intersection of the pommel and the hilt *significant*... that cross... (*Pause.*)

I will take it up. I will protect that which was given to my keeping... with my life. So help me God. And so find happiness. Thank you.

Pierce *sits amidst applause. The* M.C. *rises.*

M.C.: And now a... (*Aside.*) Did we do the...?

Assistant (*Aside*): Yes.

M.C. (*To the hall*): A Friend of our Friends, a friend of *ours*, and, *in* this time, a man who, as the Gen'ral said, is not afraid to make allegiance known: Joe Brown.

Amidst applause Joe Brown *goes to the podium, assembles his notes.*

Joe: Thank you. Thank you all. Esteemed hosts, Brothers, Pals... I am reminded of a guy in Europe, a ballplayer as it happens. In the War, he's in Pigalle in Paris. He sees this hooker. A gorgeous... piece of ass... legs up to... *young*, alright? The... goes up to her—three words of French— he goes, "Combien?" She answers him, this rapid stream, he don't know what she, "blagadelablahbegela..." He says, "Lentement! Lentement!"... and she says, "Oui!" But I'll try to be brief.

Nineteen-nineteen Arnold Rothstein, "A.R." to his friends, Hotel Ansonia, New York. Dad was in, I believe, the Rag Trade... many of them *were*... son of a *devout* man, son... of course, a disappointment to him. Saw the movie? Bit the father says "kaddish," his son is dead? A dead son. Not that bad, but almost... (*Pause.*)

A *multi*-millionaire, I'm talking nineteen-ten, nineteen-fifteen, in there, no, or small income tax.

Here's the thing:

Comiskey, as we know, perhaps the finest team ever seen in professional baseball; what's the average? Six, five or six thousand bucks a year he's paying to men who, they went *elsewhere* could start at three times that. Ballplayers getting twice that, mediocre men, easily, he's starving them.

Days of the Reserve Clause. Means you work for me or you don't work. Virtual indentureship. The men were riled. Eddie Cicotte, Shoeless Joe Jackson, legends in their time.

Men up against the... wives, et cetera... *up* against the wall. National Pastime. On the one hand, everything for show, nothing for the... but nothing for the Boys.

Team riled, unhappy... tried an abortive strike, which didn't... Rothstein comes to them. Our largest Gambler. "Put it in the Tank," he goes. "You lay down for the Cincinnati Reds..."

Someone brings him water.

Thank you...
    The... what is this?

Waterbearer: Water.

Joe: Thank you. Rothstein. "You throw the Series and you'll never have to work ag..." (*Drinks water.*) Now. Okay. The time the series comes about it's seven-to-five Sox, six-to-five and *pick* 'em, even money, seven-to-five Reds, *eight*-to-five Reds. The word is, Cincinnati players calling out the Sox: "Is it true that you threw the game?" The rest is history.

Now: whence this seemingly new concept of advocacy for athletes? You might say nineteen-nineteen Blacksocks. You might say... in that same year, the Actors Union, faced with a... *another* strike. That same year. You... faced with a trans... faced with a transitional, I think we might say... between, on the one, concepts of *serfdom*... (let's not balk at...) the idea that a man may indenture others, may, in effect, own that work; and, on the other hand, let's say, a Socialist State eschewing property entire... where... the work of the individual... we understand... what have...? What have we...? Between the...? Between the two: A Free Market. Which, al...? redounds to the benefit of...? Well:

The Blacksocks said what? Abso...? Ridden by guilt, nonetheless...

The in...

But could not: Chuck Comiskey (field bears his name today) "I...I'm the owner. They belong to me. I'll pay 'em what I want. That's what I'll pay 'em." (*Pause.*)

What I would like you for *tomorrow* to:

Rationalize the...so we do not say, because I know that this is...many of you do. Others have spoken here about avoiding zero-sum.

"I win/you lose," strategic, though, in speaking for your man, from time to time, we *must*...aaaand, we know, from, as an *exercise*, your: At the strike, *during* the strike, given intransigent behavior on the owners...with *Rothstein*, and with the Grand Jury: to represent *cogently, concisely*, as *Churchill* said: "Muster your arguments upon one side of a sheet of paper." To determine.

One: what it is that my client wants. And, again, to employ, as we heard yesterday, the Method of Parameter...

Two: how do I Get It?

Or, 'f you will: tactics and strategy.

Now: also: for each one of you...and I'd like a paper...

During the strike, the proposed strike, and, after the *scandal*, to present and defend Comiskey's position as the owner of the club.

A questioner on the floor raises his hand.

Yes.

Questioner: Was the club wholly owned?

Joe: Wholly owned by Comiskey. Yes.

Another Questioner.

Questioner II: How long should the paper be?

Joe: You're representing a man. How long should your fight be? (*Pause.*)

The Romans had a law, the name of which now escapes me, and you've heard of it before, that the test, the prime test of *negligence* in *agency* was this: put as a question to a reasonable man, eh? Did the agent prosecute his client's interests *better* than he would have acted for his own. The name of that law was?

Man in hall: Lex agencia.

Joe: Thank you. Mr. Sloan... ?

Joe retires to his seat, another man takes his place at the podium.

Sloan (*Pause*): When we get home we will find things have changed. At once, at once things change and our *view* of them alters. So that a Static State is an illusion.

Many will say "Where have you...where have you been?"

The rage that they feel at *not* having been there will express itself in...doomed to loneliness, then, many will deny the fact of love. If you will. In Australia we heard that returning troops, taunted with innuendos of our own men opened fire on them.

Men from the Great War. Sitting in a garden, Years, or thought they did...remembering what? Our own George *Patton*, who slapped that Jewish Boy...your *wives*...

Your...on return, who would cry "Embrace Me." Or "Share your thoughts with me. Share...your innermost being."

In a happier time.

Governed by Code.

A man would compartmentalize his life. Now: in a world ruled by war. Vast and horrific weapons, they tell us, loom on the horizon. Huge bombs capable of destroying a City Block. We have seen gas, and the machine gun, and *tanks.* (*Pause.*) And armored...

Once, arms swathed, a faceplate, young men fought for Honor. In the Dueling Schools, and once, in Japan, where day and night, wrong and right, a man and his State, his God, his conscience were distinct...but not now. And when you go home you will find things have changed.

Be of good faith with your faith. Trust in God.

The things which you see, which transpire, are *real*. Though they are frightening, and we may say that *you* are the apparition. As you are. Locked in a prison. Locked... one day as any day the concerns of that day obliterate... remember: at your death you will say *happiness* was just those days. Friendship, comradeship, camaraderie, love, competition... in an orderly... this saying: What is *constant* in the world? *I* am.

A pause. He takes his seat. The M.C. *stands behind the podium.*

M.C.: Thank you. (*Pause.*) Thank you. (*Pause.*) I think that's ...oh! We have ann...?

Assistant: Yes.

M.C.: We have announcements.

Assistant (*Stands at his place*): Several of you have asked about the picnic.

You are free to bring whomever you like. They need *not*...

M.C.: ...the price includes the...

Assistant: ...yes. The price is for you and a friend. You must...

M.C.: ...*any* friend, that would be...

Assistant: ...your *wife*, your *sweetheart*. A friend, an acquaintance, *any*...but you must, as there is the one ticket, you must present it *together*.

M.C.: ...at the...

Assistant: ...at...

M.C.: ...at the Gate.

Assistant: At the gate. Yes.

M.C.: Now: We:

Assistant: One more.

M.C.: I'm sorry.

Assistant: We've been given an opportunity to buy...you

saw the list on the board...many items of surplus from Bartell.

He's giving us twenty percent off—the list price is on the board. You have 'til the first, and I *urge* you, if you've looked at the list, take advantage of this, it's a once-in-a-lifetime offer.

From the floor.

Questioner II: What's on the list?

Assistant: The whole "K" series.

Questioner II: And the "102"?

Assistant: You'll have to check, but I believe it is. (*To* M.C.:) Alright.

M.C.: Did you...?

Assistant: Oh. (*Pause.*) (*Checks papers.*)

The family of John Murray...many of you knew John. John died in South America with the Green Division last month. (*Pause.*)

Katy has asked that we, to those who knew him—we have a list of his personal effects...(*He refers to list.*) His battle ribbons, a...his Zippo lighter with a crest of the One Hundred Ninth.... His Browning Hi-Power...which I believe is the one which he carried in Africa.

(*Pause.*)

Many of you who knew him...(*Pause.*) Who...(*Pause.*) Well. The list is on the board, the items are for sale. The proceeds go to his family. Thank you. (*He sits.*)

M.C.: To you all; *thank* you all. For making this the success it has been.

Let us say, as we always say:
Good Luck, Good Weather,
Bright at Dawn.
We step where those have stepped before.
A Happy Heart.
Strong shoulders to the wheel.
What is the password?

All: Answer to the Call.

M.C.: What is the Call?

All: Willing to serve.

M.C. (*Arranging his papers*): Until we meet again.

The Spanish Prisoner

One

A: I have never met a beach bum who is interesting. Their life is devoted to rest.

B: Nothing wrong with rest.

A: No. There is nothing wrong with rest. And there is nothing wrong with French pâté. I do not like it. There is a time in one's life one learns to say this: *balance*, as a principle of nature, is attractive and we see it is essential and we see it is a primal force, that all things *tend* toward rest. As I get older I see also for those who *cannot* eschew the world another force is *personality*—personality, which is to say not, *not* those quirks, those random... *shiftings* caused by tension—not those extraneous... those dissipations of our energy, our silver cig, our cigarette cases, our our our our inabilities our (*Pause.*) Our... our... there is a point where we cannot confront our longings—our desire turns *inward*, and we then begin, we, to dissimulate. Our poses with the smoke, a silken dressing gown, the smoke rising, as in a photo in the nineteen... there are other things; we say "genetic," learned, I don't know... sages said culture is not, it is not biologically inheritable. I always thought that that was trash. I did not find it true. *Today* they say: perhaps it is, and a whole *area*... the whole of, say, a certain culture, or or, culture, or... or... anthropology... all our life we were taught to escape the teachings of our senses and accept a ... to accept a... *unimpassioned* view of the world. (*Pause.*) In which we live so short a time... and called this *science*. And we raised it. On an *altar*, and we died from it, while the world... (*Pause.*) And I was saying there is something else which I call "personality" which is the, if we say we are put here to, as bees in a hive, to build a, to *cooperate* ... and if we say nature has not *deserted* us, and if we use our senses and look at the world, of which we are a part, and whose laws we are subject to, then we see this: that there *is* order; that we are a *part* of it—(how little and in spite of our...

B: ...our inabilities...

A: ...as little as we can discern it...) And as *bees* are separated by their traits, so are *we*—(*Pause.*) One, so, for *this* ...Another for *that*...Building, planning, (*Pause.*) Dreaming. In this hell in which we live. Where we have warped, where a warped, with...(*Pause.*) all turned to one—the sole gift which we...I will not say endorse, for it goes *so, so* far be...*accept*. And the rest, we say the test of *life*, the final: THE WILL TO EXPLOIT.

We, that, not only we say the *excellent* man, but, but we *all*...*whomever* does not possess this must die, because there is too little. In a more leisurely, in a historically, or an imaginary realm, or that realm of the mind—in a book or a phantasy, a perfect spot, a spot of rest.

But not here.

And I can not choose to do it. Much as I...

And I do not.

Two

C: The galleon.

D: Was...?

C: Where was I...?

D: About the...

C: Alright. The galleon, a man in...

D: The Escorial.

C: With papers. Sitting in the, say, half dark not, if you've never been there, in the dusk. An oblique...

D: ...a half-light.

C: A slanting light.

D: You, well, it *is*. It *is* red. And you *can*, you can, as much as they...You *can* smell it, and it is the same as the...

C: As the manuscripts.

D: *Today*, when everything, when paper, most of all, you

see, the idea that it cannot decompose is *monstrous.*

C: It is monstrous.

D: In the...? You were...?

C: The Escorial. A map proclaiming, fifteen forty-two, The Croja Abajo. En route to Spain, en route to, coming home to Spain. Laden with, as they conquered them. As they were conquered, and you can not read between the lines, and, curiously...(*Pause.*) Curiously...

D: You're saying?

C: Because they had enslaved, is what I came to—that terror, suppressed which we felt. We saw it as boredom, even among the ruins, though, and stricken by a majesty, and one can not suppress an awe, a *modern* awe of archi... or, we say, "construction" even then, the piety we feel for Greece was not there. Only dread, and it was hidden, I say, for the *thought* was: "If it..." "*As* it happened to them, so to us ..." the obverse of the coin, then, was, of course...

D: It was Madrid.

C: I say it was. It *was* Madrid, for sitting in that room, there was no terror. There was scholarly...

D: ...yes...

C: ...And repose, but no, and so we *look* back. And we say *they* could not feel, Nor know, Five hundred years ago. Four hundred years ago...and, perhaps, (*Pause.*) No...

D: You were going to say that it was cursed.

C: I don't know that I...The. The *land.* For, if they could, then so could we, but in the *heat.* In the *dusk,* we could not, and the walls were of *stone,* you know.

    The lattice...(*Pause.*) As I *sit* here—I see a pattern on the page, and the old tints. The *drawings* on the map. *Old* script.

D: ...you had electric light.

C: Of course, and it was, green glass shades. It threw, it threw...there...(*Pause.*)

D: Croja Abajo.

C: Lost it, quite right, and it was, too. It, lost in the, yes, we, in the (*Pause.*) "In the year *of*..."

In fifteen forty-three. The *lading* bill—the...papers that she had. A copy of her...

D: What?

C: Of her...what? Of her *sailing* orders. Four years earlier. It all...I'm sure that it will disappear. It all was there. Through all the...(*Pause.*) They've kept it. For whom? For whom? But for me—I asked myself. Who after me? Who before? (*Pause.*)

Who before me?

The records that we keep.

The latitudes. What were you going to learn? Plotted positions of her *captain*?

Why?

There was, *this* was the...(*Pause.*) The...*this, this*... *this*...the *hurricane* the *dates* said, the direction of her, that is to say, she, en route to her final port-of-call...how did it catch her, if the dates did not conform, and how were, the winds, where did she, where did she try to run, for it said that she did, where did she seek that shelter? What were the things she had done before? That he had done, where had he taken her?

A map upon the table.

A...accentuate to what? To their, to tr...re...a feeling ..."Play the Black..." Finally what is it? Just a feeling, buttressed by...(*Pause.*) Science. By Experience?

To make us less afraid.

"The ship is down," they'd tried to find her for...They'd tried to find her for...The records had been opened since ...Before the war, and then after the war. Who'd sat like me, and looked upon...The records of their trip...the... sketches of the artifacts—but not the gold.

D: Others had gotten gold.

C: And lived in, you see it...the cruelty of the Middle Age. *Especially* here—cursed by...We can see that there are cursed folk...I thought: What does it mean?

The plagues of Egypt.

Surely they afflicted... *this* is the: the power to see did not lessen their danger. For the Jews, though, it does not say, but it says they were not giv'n a sign until the final, so they must have lived with those ten plagues, and, stricken by them, too, looked for...(*Pause.*) They...(*Pause.*)

I thought about the gash of, the blood on the door, what did it mean, and it was *obviously* a...an...*imbalance*. Differences in diet, *some* thing a...an...an...in, say a, a intestinal malady which they were not subject to. And the Egyptians died and the Jews lived and *though* subject to the plagues of that life they said it was a sign. So, here, the opposite. A curse. A heaviness. The *weight* of gold...and, as an element...for, certainly, all...if we look, as I looked in that room, protected by the walls, by heat, by the, "and *blest* by the dust of the crumbling manuscripts..." *Protected*...And I saw all things are literal.

They mean exactly what they seem to mean. (*Pause.*) Those men coming back were never to reach home. They were infected. They were weighted down, the same god which had sent the gold which sent the storm.

Although others had gone before.

Although these...

And reached home (*Pause.*)

And reached home with their prize.

Which formed the basis of their fortune.

Three

F: You see: one needn't have confidence, because it is also possible to lose—so there is a result to your actions *whatever* you do. (*Pause.*) And you cannot combat human misery.

G: Who cannot?

F: A boy died. In Alabama. In some southern state. A black boy in a *state* where, they had said, and they needn't have said it...

G: Niggers.

F: In a word as things that *we* would say, that *they* would censure. You would say, "A conquered people." As they were. A love of... of, a tradition of honor, true or not, as all traditions are. A history of loss. *One* aspect of white males at the door, at the schoolyard door, barring a frightened five-year-old, a black girl in a...

G: In a yellow dress.

F: Thirty years later in that state, in that same state a boy who, as a student had worked for the Governor, a black boy a white, a, Louisiana...

G: What dif...?

F: Well, that's what we say, you see: Who possess the prerogative to say: Your History, your Mores, your... finally, what makes you different is, and, do not say "A Luxury..." But, a *stupidity*, a *trick*, and, fostered on you by the: Too much *time*...too much time on your hands— as all culture—*Heat*. The need to...or, otherwise, say, say, "The Great Chain of Being," if, in England, but not *here*, because here what we are is without hist...and things change, and some things do not change. (*Pause.*) But, to *Western* eyes, which is to say, the minds of people from the *North*, rapacious, sons steeped in the Blazonment...a knight rides out and, you know him by his shield, or as the Bard says, "Reputation." We say, "Advertising," yes, an English shirt, a French whore, a dumb cracker, a nig, any of those things one said, one said that only shallow people

Cannot judge by first impressions.

In that Southern State, however, a boy died, a black boy, *who* everyone said, I don't know, some...some...a

G: Some sharecropper's son.

F: The no, son, of no, son of a doctor...a poor boy, HE WOULD BE PRESIDENT. Everyone said in twenty years. Who worked at this, who worked at that, at those accomplishments, which, here below (*Pause.*)

Here below...

And one says, "What are they trying to Hide?"

What overcome? As I would overcome, or they, if I had,

with those, as reported, twenty-hour days, but they said, "Here..." and changed the lives of everyone who came in contact with the boy, "Perhaps here we have found an instance of a perfect man." *Why* did he die so young? What would it matter had he lived, who moved so many by his ...and the *answer* is...the answer is: That human misery is lifted only by this—it would, it would, it would seem... O...by an act of love, who knew him knew that, and I thought: "How sad." An outpouring...a *sainted* reminiscence of the boy, over the years...now, *who* could keep that up? How it would, how inevitably, induce shame, induce guilt in those...how do we know he only had one parent...

G: one...?

F: One parent living.

G: How do we know that?

F: I'm...I think that I read it. I'm not, what I meant to say: It seems...what strikes me in the boy is, of c...is the mythic

G: The Good Die

F:...excuse me: Maj...the maj...the *majesty* of it. Its strength come (*Pause.*) From repetition. It is a tale that we know. The psych, the psycho...the unconscious aspect of one parent dead, a man on one leg who *overcomes* his... whose internal strength who...when the *governor* came He said the Good Die Young. He cried. (*Pause.*) You felt *here* was a good man. You felt everyone who read the piece was better for it. Oneself most of all. One wished one knew him. We would have slighted him, of course. We would have cut him. (*Pause.*) Maybe not.

G: We would have cut him on the street.

F: Well. That doesn't...no. That doesn't alter the power of the tale. Here is another one: the woman trying to escape, A southern Clime. A dictator. Her Father's Fortune confiscated. She, herself, in fear. For her life. Flees. The documents, the gold itself, inside a sealed trunk. The trunk in safety, inaccessible except to her. But it can be located. Her life can be saved. The man who aids her escape will reap her love and share her fortune.

Who would not support her?

And so he does so. You know the rest.

Two Conversations

Two Conversations, Two Scenes, and *Yes But So What* were first presented at The Ensemble Studio Theatre in New York as part of the Marathon 1983 Festival of One-Act Plays on May 6, 1983, with the following cast directed by Curt Dempster:

Two Conversations	*Two Scenes*	*Yes But So What*
Dan Ziskie	Peter Maloney	David Rasche
James Rebhorn	Ann Spettel	Frank Girardeau
Deborah Hedwall	Diane Venora	
Melodie Somers		
Peter Phillips		
Jude Ciccolella		

After dinner conversation. A and B, two women. C and D, two men.

One

C (*Hands* D *a note*): Read it.

D: "I can't come today be..."

A: Who is this?

C: That's our house...

D: It's the house cleaner...

C: Read it.

D: "I can't come today because something has happened to me." Is this the...?

C: Yes.

D: Last week...?

C: Yes.

D: He...he came, he came, didn't...

C: He came to leave the note.

D: I'd...do you mind if I tell...

A: You two have the same...?

C: We gave him to them. He...

D: He was a wonderful...

C: You've seen him here.

A: No. I don't...

B: What does he look like?

D: Thirty-five. Small, thin, balding...

C: This man does such fantastic work...

B: What hap...?

C: *Apparently*...well, tell them about...

D: I got a phone call. (*Pause.*) I was at the office, I was between...this was, when...?

C: Last...

D: Last *Monday*. He'd been at my house Sat...

C: He...yes. Yes. Saturday.

D: Monday I get a call. "I have to confess something. I have something important to talk..."

A: Had you talked be...

D: We'd never been, no. No. He'd never... "How are *you?*" The *weather*...so on. *So:*

C: ...this happened to him, too, four years ago. When he...

D: When he first came to...

A: ...where did he...?

D: Up...

C: ...when he...

D: Upstate.

C: When he, yes. When he first started with...I had to call his father. He came in...

A: This...

D: Yes.

A: This is four *years* ago...

D: Yes.

C: ...He came in one day. I came in. (*Pause.*) He was sitting on the floor. His *shirt* was off. He was just sitting there. He'd been there all day. And he saw nothing unusu...

D: That's the *thing*...that's the *thing*...that's the *point*... that's what I always say. As...wait. As *crazy*...as *unhappy* as we think we are, the line between psychotic and neurotic is not a thin line. (*Pause.*) It's not a thin divider at all. It's like. I think it's like...It's like the difference between... (*Pause.*) It's, um, it's like the difference between competence and talent. (*Pause.*)

A: What do you think causes...

D: ...between...

A: What do you think causes it?

D: Psy...? I...I don't know. *Genetic*...Um. (*Pause.*) Diet...

C: An imbalance of some kind...

D: Yes. An imbalance. Yes. That isn't pred...

B: He worked for both of you...?

D: That isn't predicated...

C: Yes...

D: On some mistaken *notion*. Do you know what I mean?

C: That's much *deeper*...

A: People living in their own dream don't know that they're in a dream. (*Pause.*)

C: Absolutely.

D: *Um. Now:* an example: If you were *unhappy*, you could *say* so. You'd say, "God, I hate myself." Or...

A: Mm hmm...

D: "God, I'm fat..."

A: Mm hmm...

D: *He* doesn't *know* that. He is in a *dream.*

A: He'd been committed before?

D: Yes.

C: When he first worked for us.

B: Um hm.

C: Tell them last week.

D: Last week: last *Monday*, he called me at work. "I have to talk to you." Did you see...what *was* that...?

C: Some *German* picture...

D: Some *German* thing. Where the same thing happened...

C: ...I don't know the name of it...

D: He'd stolen two decks of cards. (*Pause.*) He called me. But I couldn't talk. "I have to talk to you. I have to confess. I've taken your cards."

C: ...he asked *me*...

D: Yes...

C: I said, "Don't call. You see...You're putting him in an..."

D: It was a cry for *help.*

A: *Certainly.*

C: "...in an embarrassing..."

D: I mean the *cards* were worth, what? Two dollars...

C: In an embarrassing position. Yes. It was a...

D: Well, that's what I *told* him. That was the...

A: ...the only way he had...

D: Yes.

C: I told him to for...

D: He told him to forget it. Then he called *me.* Then *Jim* called. I told him...

C: Wait. Tell them about the a...

D: Oh yes. He says "Did you...?"

C: ...that *German* film...

D: "Did you see the..." um...um..."No, why...?" "Because your *ace* is missing." (*Pause.*)

A: That was in some film?

D: Yes. It signified...I don't know...

C: "You're in danger," he says.

D: "Jim...Jim..."

C: I said it was just his way of at...

D: Of attracting attention. *Certainly*...

B: *Wait.* (*Pause.*) He took *playing* cards? (*Pause.*)

D: Yes. (*Pause.*)

B: *Why?* (*Pause.*) Why, do you think? (*Pause.*)

D: I don't know.

B: *Because* of the movie. (*Pause.*)

A: What do you mean?

B: So he could take the ace and say he had a, you know... (*Pause.*)

D: A reason to call *up*.

B: Yes. (*Pause.*)

D: Hm. Well. You may be right.

C: When this happened before he was in for six months. When he came *out*...

D: He did such a marvelous job...

C: This house was *spotless*. There was nothing you would not *eat* off of. Seriously...

D: He treated it as an art.

C: He *did*. Yes. That's exactly how he treated it.

D: He treated it as an art, he was *inventive*...

C: ...yes.

D: ...he was...

C: ...he...

D: ...he was *dependable*...

C: When he got out he *came* to me and asked me would I try him again. Which of course I *did*...

A: And he was fine?

C: Yes.

A: Mm.

C: Fade out, fade in...

D: Four years later.

C: Mm.

D: So: when he *called* I said:

C: He said to call *me*.

D: I couldn't talk to him...

C: Waal, it couldn't have helped in any case. (*Pause.*) He...

A: He didn't want to *confess*...He

D: He wanted to be helped. Yes.

C: He...he *came* to me. He said, "I need a rest." I said, "Jim. You don't need a rest. You need serious help." (*Pause.*)

B: I'm sure that he felt incredibly lonely or he would never have done what he did. (*Pause.*) I know I would feel very lonely if that happened to *me*. (*Pause.*)

C: *Well.* (*Pause.*) He asked me to call his father...

D: The fellow, all his friends, he picks them up at four A.M. on the streets...

C: ...and so I *did*, and he...

D: ...this is the interesting part:

C: He says, "He's no good. He never was any good. He's a bum. He always..."

D: This, this is his father talking...

C: "And he always was. He never should have come down to New *York*. Since he *got* there he..."

D: *Mmm...?*

C: "He's done *nothing?*" I said. "Sir. Your son has a thriving *business*. On the *contrary:* he's...I've seen his *accounts*. He's *organized*. (*Pause.*) He's *meticulous*...he does his job *superlatively*...(*Pause.*) He's *reliable*...he's *not* a bum. He's *ill*. (*Pause.*) He's *ill*. He needs *help*. (*Pause.*)

A: Did the father come down?

C: *No.* We took him to...

D: We took him to Bellevue. (*Pause.*)

A: Will they take good care of him there?

D: Yes. I think they will. Yes.

C: Yes. They will. (*Pause.*)

A: Do you think that's treatable?

C: Yes. I think that it is. Yes. And I don't, I'll tell you something, I don't think it's in the *mind*, either...

B: What?

C: Schizophrenia.

A: Schiz...

C: No. I think it's cau...

A: It isn't in the *mind*...?

C: I'm saying that it's *cause*...I think the *cause* is not. (*Pause.*) That the true *cause* of it is not *trauma*...or...Infantile *trauma* or...say what I'm saying...

D: That the cause is something simple. *Diet* or genetic...

C: *Yes.*

D: Genetic pre...

A: Predisposition.

D: Yes.

C: And I'll tell you what *else:* I think *someday someone's* going to find how to *cure* schizophrenia with a...say, with a simple *touch*...with...(*Pause.*) with...a small change in *diet*...(*Pause.*) With...

D: Mm hmm...

C: ...with a *pressure* point...with...

D: ...with a simple *touch.* (*Pause.*)

C: Yes. (*Pause.*) Absolutely. (*Pause.*)

A: Will he be in there long?

C: I don't know.

A: Will you take him back when he comes out?

C: Certainly.

D: Absolutely.

C: Absolutely. (*Pause.*)

Two

After dinner conversation. A and B, two men.

A: ...the way *I* understand it...the way *I* understand it... *I'll* tell you what the *Antichrist* is...

B: What?

A: I'll tell you, and I believe it will come. Although I *don't* believe we've seen it yet. When we'll *see it*, when we'll *see* it is in the *hard*...in the *true*...eh? In the *true, true* hard times. And what I think the *Antichrist* is is, the way that we can understand it's if we say "The False Girlfriend." (*Pause.*) Mm. When one is ready to be *married.* Then you say that *this* one has something *unique* which until now you *longed* for but...

B: ...yes...

A: But you couldn't *find.* So now you've *found* it, now you can...

B: Um hmm...

A: Get *married.* (*Pause.*)

B: So now you can get married.

A: But it's just the *time* is right. That's all. The time is right; and *when* it is you *see* someone and say, "She is the One." Now: Full of our old habits, the person that we see *first*— like a *policeman.* He sees the streets differently from a *cab* driver...they both see different things—so when we're *ready*...

B: Mm...

A: To *wed*—it could be our old *habits* cause our *sight* to fasten on...

B: Uh huh...

A: A...

B: ...the false...

A: No. Not necessarily *false.* Yes. False. In a way. In that all that's *wrong,* finally, is that she...she's not the right— put in her place as, simply, as a "woman," *fine.* But as the girl for *you,* no. No. To *marry*? No. Because you're caught in your "pre-courtship..." No. "Pre-marriage courtship context." Your *sight*...(*Pause.*) Your body says "wed." But your soul, your, no, your *habits* still in that outmoded mode of *thinking.* So she's wrong. She's the wrong one. Although the *time* is right. You break up with this person. You find someone *new*. You *marry* and you say "Now how *extraordinary* that I found *two* such..."

B: ...yes...

A: ...and, if you *think*, you reason back and you see that it was only the *time* was right. Just like a *flower*. (*Pause.*) That's all. So, with the *Antichrist*...it's just an...here's where I think the new test...it's...

B: ...the New Testament...

A: ...it's *brilliant*. What it *is* is, finally, I think, I could be wrong, perhaps not in *entirety*, but perhaps *so*, I don't know. What it is is allegory for *marriage*. (*Pause.*) The *Christ*, the *Antichrist*...*reunion*...

B: You're saying it's pri...

A: What?

B: It's primarily a ho...

A: A what?

B: A homosexual relationship.

A: What is?

B: I don't mean a ho...I mean a homosexual *romance*...

A: No. (*Pause.*) *Perhaps* it is. (*Pause.*) No. Because we're... Ah. Because we're waiting for that *man*...

B: For that one man...

A: No. Perhaps so, Huh. (*Pause.*) Huh. (*Pause.*) What are you saying? (*Pause.*)

B: That it's a homosexual romance.

A: Huh. (*Pause.*)

B: No. I'm not saying that. I'm asking if...

A: If *I* implied that.

B: Yes.

A: If the New Testament...(*Pause.*) No. I don't think so. (*Pause.*) You're...wait a second. I said it's an...

B: ...it's an allegory...

A: ...it's an allegory for...

B: ...mmm hmm...

A: But what *you're* saying

B: Yes. For marriage. But it's not a reconciliation with the...

A: With the *Earth*...

B: Yes.

A: With the, um, um, with the *mother* figure...no.

B: But...

A: Yes. Mmm. With the...yes...

B: Yes. With the...

A: But with the *father*. (*Pause.*)

B: It's not a hetero...

A: No...

B: If we...

A: Yes. Taken as a romance. No. (*Pause.*) Mm. Striving for ...(*Pause.*) No. (*Pause.*)

Wait a second. (*Pause.*) Now; what are we: what are we ...what are we *saying* here: Let's step back...(*Pause.*) That Christianity is...(*Pause.*) I started off, I said that the *Antichrist* is The False Girlfriend...

B: Is *like* the false...

A: But it would be the false *Boyfriend* is what you're saying. (*Pause.*) You're saying that the whole religion's basically an apology for homosexuality

B: I don't think that I'm saying that.

A: Well. It's the logical extension of your...A reunion with the *Father*. A refusal to accept the...um...the weight of ...hetero...*essentially*...wait...wait a second: *mate*, have *children, bequeath*...the seed bank...pass on your, um, and *die*. Essentially the hetero...and what *you're* saying ...well. Well, yes. Um. And living *forever*. (*Pause.*) That You will live forever. It's a, yes, it's basically a refusal to *change. Continence*...um, we are assured that if we plight our troth to the *father* figure we will not d... which is, um, to say we will not grow *up*. We will not grow *old*. Ha. So we have discovered the... wait, we have discovered the Perfect Man. We fall in love with him, and we will not grow old. Yes. It's a homosexual romance. Yes. If we, what? If we *sufficiently*, if we love him with all our *hearts* (*Pause.*) Um. (*Pause.*) It really has nothing to do with *women, does* it? (*Pause.*) No. (*Pause.*) Mmm. (*Pause.*) And his attachment to his *mother*! Well, no not *his*, but *ours*...um...we can't... we can't *divorce* ourselves from... Oh! Oh! Oh! and the Weak, Absent *Father*! Hm! The Father Cuckolded! The impotent... the failure of the marriage... Ha! Ha! (*Pause.*) Ha! (*Pause.*) Ha! Oh! Oh! I've got to... (*Gets up.*) excuse me...

B: Will I see you...?

A: Yes. I'll call you tonight.

Two Scenes

One

A: Give me one.

B: Here is a one.

A: Give me a two.

B: Here is two.

A: Give me three.

B: I don't have three.

A: Give me a two.

B: Here is two.

A: Give me a one.

B: Here is one.

A: Give me a four.

B: I have four.

A: Give me a five.

B: Here is a five.

A: Give me a six.

B: Six.

A: Give me seven.

B: Yes.

A: Eight.

B: Yes.

A: Give me nine.

B: I don't have nine.

A: Give me eight.

B: Yes.

A: Give me another eight.

B: Eight.

A: Give me ten.

B: Here is ten.

A: Let me have ten again.

B: Ten.

A: Give me twelve.

B: Here is twelve.

A: Nine through twelve.

B: Yes.

A: Eight.

B: Yes.

A: ...that was eight through twelve?

B: It was. We don't have nine. I mean "ten through twelve."

A: Yes.

B: ...or "nine through twelve," but we don't have nine.

A: Yes. Give me eight.

B: Eight again?

A: Yes.

B: Here is eight.

A: And give me five.

B: Five.

A: One through three.

B: Yes.

A: No. *Three.* Is that right?

B: That is right.

A: Two alone.

B: Two.

A: Five.

B: Five.

A: Fifteen.

B: Yes.

A: Eleven.

B: Yes.

A: Eleven and five.

B: Yes.

A: *Two* eleven and five.

B: Yes.

A: *Three* eleven and five. Make that four...scrub that. Forget that. Give me six.

B: Six.

A: Six and five.

B: Go.

A: Six two five and five.

B: Yes.

A: One.

B: Yes.

A: Good. That's alright.

B: Are you done?

A: I think so. Yes. Thank you.
   Um, um, um. No. I think that's it. I'm done. Thank you. I'm finished. Fine. That's fine. That's very good; in fact, I'm happy with it. (*Pause.*) That's very good.

Two

Speaker: Up. Everyone up. *Up*...
   That's right.
   Down slowly.
   Down.
   Now left. Left. Left.
   And left.

Now right. *Hold*...hold it...up...now center...left. Left left.

Now down. Now left again and hold.

Return.

Now down.

Now up again. Now hold.

And right right right.

Now down and *hold*.

Now cross.

And back again.

Now *cross*...

Now *center*...*out*...and *hold it*...out again...wait for it...out...and *Good*!

(*Pause.*)

In. Now hold. And *left.* Now hold. And *in* now hold. And *right* now hold.

And *in* now hold. And *left* now hold...and *in* now hold and *yes* and *out* and *left* now hold and *down.*

(*Pause.*)

Good.

(*Pause.*)

Good.

(*Pause.*)

Very Good.

(*Pause.*)

Wait. (*Pause.*) Wait. (*Pause.*) Down...(*Pause.*)
Down...(*Pause.*) Good! (*Pause.*) Good. (*Pause.*)
Good.

Yes But So What

Two men.

A: She lost a tack I said, "Well take your shoes off..." Hey? "...you'll find it in one second."

B: ...bitch

A: ...man, all day long...

B: What did she need it for?

A: The fuck *I* know, when I come home...

B: ...*hunh*...

A: ...sit around all day...

B: ...and then her *father* died...

A: It's not her father, man...

B: ...no?

A: It's not.

B: Who, I mean, it was, was it, who was it?

A: It was her father's *brother*...

B: ...*what* is that...? Her...

A: *No.*

B: How come? It's not her, *what*...?

A: Her *uncle*.

B: Yeah.

A: It's *not* that, he was *step*, something...she *called* him, she told you her *father* died?

B: I think I heard that wrong.

A: She *called* him Uncle. Uncle *Charlie* some like that...

B: Her *uncle*...

A: What excuse is that...? "Who broke the plate...?" "The *girl* broke it."

B: What plate...?

A: Some...I don't know..."Ask the *girl*," hey, *fuck*, I'm gone out to ask the girl, "Yes meester," all that shit...

B: What is she?

A: Some, I don't know...from *Colombia*, somewhere...

B: What was the plate?

A: The plate? That my grandmother... *you've* seen it.

B: A blue...

A: No.

B: On the wall?

A: Up on the wall. Yeah. *Hanging* there...

B: Uh-huh.

A: I come in, on the wall, "What *is* that...?" *Knick* knacks...

"Where's the plate...?" "The girl broke it," hey, I don't give a fuck. Don't laze *around* all day. Don't with your *T.V.* show, then lay this copping, copping, this, uh, copping *out* on me. *Tell* me. That's what I would ask. "Well, I dropped the *tack*..." Well *find* it. Huh? Unless what does this *indicate* when I come home? *I* don't know...something. *Huh?*

B: Yeah.

A: What?

B: I don't know.

A: Some, some, she's dis*satis*fied. *Some*thing. Some *deep* ...but....Or let me try *this* on you: Broad in the bar:

B: Which one?

A: The looked-like-some...amateur *dyke* alright? The no-tits ten year old, the *broad* alright?

B: You like that *young*...

A: ...she wasn't that young, what I'm saying what she *looked:* Some broads, I've *thought* this, I've su*spec*ted this, you tell me I'm insane, I'm lookin' this broad in the bar...

B: ...the *willow* broad...

A: Yes. What do you...?

B: I don't mean "willow." What do I mean?

A: I don't know.

B: That *color*...

A: I don't know...

B: that...

A: What does it look like?

B: Like *yellow*.

A: I don't know. That she had *on*?

B: Yeah.

A: That she had *on*, or like in her *hair*?

B: That she had on. I *told* you...

A: On her *shirt*...?

B: *Yeah*.

A: The broad with the yellow *shirt*.

B: Yeah.

A: In the *bar*.

B: Yeah.

A: She looked like a *dyke*.

B: The young dyke...

A: Yeah.

B: Yes.

A: What about her?

B: That's the *one*.

A: Yeah. (*Pause.*) Yeah. (*Pause.*) Hey. That's *her* problem. (*Pause.*) No, that's *her* problem. D' I tell you when I went home I saw a traffic accident?

B: No.

A: Yes. I did.

B: Where?

A: Eighteenth Street.

B: When?

A: Last night.

B: When we left the bar?

A: Yes.

B: What happened?

A: Some fucker got knocked down.

B: Was he dead?

A: No. (*Pause.*)

B: No? (*Pause.*)

A: He was moving.

B: He was?

A: Yeah. (*Pause.*) They had a lot of cars. (*Pause.*) Um. They had an ambulance. (*Pause.*) You ever think that will happen to you?

B: No. (*Pause.*)

A: I do sometimes. (*Pause.*) What I'm saying that the *thoughts* that you have. (*Pause.*)

B: Huh.

A: Do you know what I mean? (*Pause.*) That the *thoughts* you have will, um, they'll, that that they come *back* to you. (*Pause.*)

B: ...uh...

A: That if you're *looking* at this poor man's got his *legs* chopped off with *glee*, some fuckin' thing, "How *happy* that I am...!" "that I'm alive," so on, or "that poor sucker with no legs...," that will come back to you. To *haunt* you. Time in, um, where was it...Newton, there was this, I knew this girl, she said that if you *do* a thing, you come *back*—I don't know if she believed that you *come* back, but if you *did*—you come back in the afterlife, you *are* that thing you scorned.

B: Like what?

A: Some sucker that you scorn. (*Pause.*) Like you make fun of a man, a *beggar*. (*Pause.*)

B: Huh...

A: *I* don't know. I think that thoughts transmit themselves.

(*Pause.*) I don't know. But I think they do. They could...
we never know the, look at *medicine*, one year, "Do this..."
The next year, "We have this *discovery*, don't do *this* go do
that." Or, "All the shit that your *grandparents* did is right,
we just found out. Because the blah blah blah and *science*."
(*Pause.*) But they were stupid anyway...

B: They could transmit themselves.

A: *Thoughts?*

B: Yes.

A: I know that. Tell that to me when I come home, because
I'm thinking of this *broad*, alright... The...

B: Yeah.

A: The *dyke* broad...

B: ... with the ass...

A: That's right, and I come... not, not *even* when I come,
before I have come in the door, alright? With, if I, I don't
know that I *did*, but *if... if* I did, if I had let's, let's say if
I'm coming in with *hostility* because of, that would be. If
I had a *desire*, alright, and I come home, and *she's*... I'm
saying: "I wish I was going home with *this* broad. *That*
would make me happy. I swear to God that it would. (*Pause.*)
It would be a simple answer to a lot of things and hurt no
one." I come in the door, and I think, "What's *stopping* me?"
the fact I'm going home to someone...

B: ... someone *else*...

A: My wife yes, and she's on the ladder with the lamp.
    I don't mean the lamp. With the *plate*... I don't mean
the plate. Having *dropped* the plate. "The girl, your *plate*
is smashed." What smashed the plate? (*Pause.*) My *hostility.*
I'm not sayin that it did. I'm not sayin it did *not*.... But
what I am *saying* is *I don't know.* (*Pause.*) That... (*Pause.*)
That... (*Pause.*) That... I think that *many* of us, alright, *much*
of the time, I may be, I, I may be, maybe I'm full, maybe,
what the hell, we all have the right to be wrong. Maybe,
I'm, uh, maybe...

B: If we...

A: ...hold on:

B: ...if we...

A: Hold on:

B: If we weren't...

A: Yeah, yeah, yeah...if we *weren't* wrong...

B: ...if...

A: If we *weren't* wrong...

B: The sci...

A: Yes. The scientific things. Yes.

B: All the, yes.

A: That's what I'm saying...

B: The...

A: ...the...

B: The *inventions*.

A: the *inventions*. Yes.

B: That...

A: *Yes.*

B: That were dis...

A: Yes. I'm saying, alright. Yes...Maybe I'm *wrong*...

B: ...all that were discovered by...

A: Well, then that fucking proves my *point*, so shut...

B: That, um...

A: Alright. Alright, that's what I'm saying. (*Pause.*) Maybe I'm, *here*, in *this*, maybe I'm *wrong*. (*Pause.*) Maybe I am. That's what I'm saying.

B: They discovered them by chance.

A: I know they did.

B: Through being wrong.

A: Well, not through being wrong exactly, no, but other people *thought* they were. (*Pause.*) Is that what you meant? (*Pause.*)

B: Yes.

A: (*Pause.*) They *themselves* were wrong. Do you know why?

B: Because they didn't take the time to...

A: Ab...

B: To...

A: Absolu...

B: I don't mean "time..."

A: No, I know what you mean.

B: "care"

A: The *care* to...

B: Yes.

A: ...That they didn't *trust* themselves.

B: They didn't *trust* themselves.

A: That's absolutely right.

B: To *see*...

A: To see the things before their nose. Or, wait a second here, to trust an *inner*...

B: Mmm.

A: To an *inner* truth...

B: ...that they had seen...

A: Eh?

B: Yes

A: An *inner* truth. (*Pause.*)

B: Yes.

A: Or a "*feeling.*" (*Pause.*) What *are* feelings...? We don't know what they are...

B: No.

A: We "feel" them...

B: Huh...

A: Big fuckin deal...

B: Yeah.

A: You know...?

B: Like *sicknesses*...

A: Who *knows* what they are...?

B: *No* one...

A: Just because we *say*...

B: ...that's right...

A: We put a *name* on...

B: ...yeah. We put a name on it, it makes us comfortable...

A: That's absolutely right.

B: What does it "mean"...?

A: *Bullshit*...

B: That's absolute...

A: It *doesn't* mean that we know what it is.

B: No.

A: *Bullshit. Bullshit. That's* all that it means.

B: Yes.

A: *Plants*...(*Pause.*) *Plants* or *flowers*...(*Pause.*) or *animals* or *thoughts*. Or *words*...what are *words*? *Words* for things, for things themselves...*bullshit* for *feelings* about things.

A: They stand in the *way*.

B: They *do*.

A: Of seeing what they are.

B: They do.

A: They're *such* bullshit...

B: They are...

A: ..."*feelings*..."

B: ...shit...(*Pause.*)

A: *Such* shit. *Such* nonsense. (*Pause.*)

B: You have to have the power to let *go*.

A: You *do.*

B: To go *beyond...*

A: To go, that's absolu...that's absolutely *right.* That's absolutely right. (*Pause.*) Something that we *say*...we put a *name* on it, and...(*Pause.*) and...(*Pause.*) and...(*Pause.*)

B:...like a *bowling* pencil...

A: I was thinking, that you're walking down the street, you have a *wrapper* of some thing. You say, "I know what I should do. I know that I should throw it in the can." So you walk toward the can. You're tossing it, alright, the while you are you're knowing that it, I'm sorry, but it's true, while you are, you know that it won't go in. You, God knows why you do it, but you, huh, as if you're playing a *joke* on yourself. One part of your mind does not know what the other, huh ...? You toss it toward the can. You *know* it won't go in. It has no chance. You, *you* aren't going back. A part of you says, "You knew that it wasn't going in the thing"...but you walk on. You say, "What kind of a *world* is it when people like *me* can *do* things like that? I could have tossed it in the can." And you walk on. You think, "I should be punished." As you cross the street you are hit by a cab.

B: Are you killed?

A: No. (*Pause.*)

B: Are you badly injured?

A: I think so. I don't know. Maybe. Maybe not, it's, well, to say you would, you would be crippled for life, on the one hand that seems harsh, you didn't throw the paper in the can. Eh? On the *other* hand, you are, so, you know, who*ever*— I'm talking about, you know in your why go *separate* them? You know you are wrong. You've done a wrong thing. Maybe ...may...(*Pause.*) maybe...(*Pause.*)

B: You want to know there is a God.

A: The guy, the wrapper.

B: That's...that's...

A: Why would you...

B: You want to know there is a...

A: Yeah, yeah, yeah. I *get* that, but why would you want to draw attention to him to yourself?

B: Behaving *badly.* (*Pause.*) You want to know there is a God, you miss the paper in the can, you don't go back. You're, um, you're *guilty, guilty*, right? You say: "The blah, blah, blah, I'm going to roast in Hell." And yeah, yeah, so there is a God. "These assholes on the, *they* don't know how bad I am... *God* does..." Why not to draw attention to your...

B: ...yes...

A: By acting *good*...well, who *knows* what is good? We're assholes. (*Pause.*) I don't know...I don't know. I don't know *anything.* (*Pause.*) The fuckin *house* salad is no good; I'll tell you what I know: The, they call it *"House* salad," it's no good; a fellow, *and*, you take out a cigar, the *other* guy hands you one of his own says "Here..." alright? "Here, smoke a *good* cigar"...it is in*var*iably a piece of shit... (*Pause.*) What else? The broad says "I never *did* this before" is lying to herself. Those are the three things that I know.

B: Does she believe it?

A: The broad?

B: Yes.

A: There's something else that I know but I forgot what it is.

B: The broad...

A: "Does she believe it?" Yes. I told you. Yes.

B: Is it true?

A: No.

VERMONT SKETCHES

Conversations with the Spirit World

Pint's a Pound the World Around

Dowsing

Deer Dogs

In the Mall

Maple Sugaring

Morris and Joe

Four of the *Vermont Sketches, Conversations with the Spirit World, Pint's a Pound the World Around, Dowsing,* and *Deer Dogs,* were first presented at The Ensemble Studio Theatre in New York as part of the Marathon 1984 Festival of One-Act Plays on May 24, 1984, with the following cast directed by Gregory Mosher:

Conversations with the Spirit World
Frank Hamilton
Colin Stinton

Pint's a Pound the World Around
W. H. Macy
Joe Ponazecki

Dowsing
Frank Hamilton
Joe Ponazecki

Deer Dogs
W. H. Macy
Colin Stinton

CONVERSATIONS WITH THE SPIRIT WORLD

Characters: Two men: Morris, James

Morris: Dowsing for the like the kid says, "What cha doin'?" Says, "I'm *dowsing.*" "What is that?" "I'm looking for this *line...*" "Line is *that?*"...*"Line I'm *looking* for..." He points. "That *purple* line...?"

James: No...

Morris: *Yes,* and by dajn if he didn't point it *out.*

James: He *saw* it...?

Morris: Well, that's what I'm *telling* you..."What are you doing?" "Dowsing for a *well...*" By God, I'm trine to get these silly *sticks* to work...

James: ...uh-huh...

Morris: S'I find this *line,* I'm trying to feel the line and Clark can *see...* I'll tell you something else: *Ivers.*

James: Now who is that...?

Morris: Say eighteen *thirty...* say eighteen, to eighteen forty-*five, fifty,* hired man up to Hayes place...

James: Uh-huh...

Morris: ...he died, *Clara* said that he didn't go *over.*

James: ...old *Hayes* farm...

Morris: The old *Hayes* farm. The *hired* man. Now: Annie, she was *young,* you know, we'd hear her *talking...*

James: ...uh-huh...

Morris: ...young folks do, a little kid, you know, a year old, she'd be *talking...*

James: She'd be talking to herself...

Morris: Uh-huh...one day, we're up there, Clara asks her who she's *talking* to. She says, "This man..."

James: Uh-huh.

Morris: So she...now, I think, *I think* what Annie says is *Clara* asks her, "What's his *name*?" Annie says "Ivan," something like that. Later it occurs to me, now where'd she get *that* from...?

James: The Russians.

Morris: ...What *I* thought. But even *so*, something she *heard*? Where would she *hear* that. I told...I remember this, I'm telling stories on my *kids*...

James: ...uh-huh...

Morris: To *Chunk*, I think it was...

James: Chunk *Kellog*.

Morris: Yes. Said, "Where she *gets* it from...some man named *Ivan*." He said, "Ask her was it Ivan she said or *Ivers*." Who he was, as I said, a *hired* man, a hundred *years* ago.

James: He die a violent death?

Morris: I don't *know*. What *Chunk* said...*yes*. *Yes*. I think he did. He, what *Chunk* said, he didn't want to go across...

James: Uh-huh...

Morris: And, to that *time* he habited the house.

James: Annie remember this?

Morris: Well, you don't *know*...

James: Uh-huh...

Morris: Whether she, what she *saw*, or the *stories*...

James: ...uh-huh...

Morris: ...you know...

James: Yes.

Morris: ...that she remembers that we'd tell. And she *described* him.

James: What'd she say?

Morris: A *man*, you know, I don't remember...*beard*

James: ...uh-huh...

Morris: A heavy *shirt*...

James: Mm. (*Pause.*)

Morris: Reason *I thought* of it, dowsing for water, and *Clark* says...

James: Well, they say ninety percent *anyone* can dowse...

Morris: ...that's right...

James: ...and a *hundred* percent all *children*.

Morris: That's right. (*Pause.*) That's right.

James: *Jean* saw something out on the hill.

Morris: What was that?

James: ...the old *sugar* lane...

Morris: Uh-huh...

James: *Dusk* one day...

Morris: When was this?

James: Last fall.

Morris: Uh-huh.

James: She got me, I was in the *bedroom*, she comes in...

Morris: What was it...?

James: She says, "A boy." (*Pause.*) A boy?
   "Out at the entrance to the *lane*."
   "Now, who would *that* be...?"
   I could tell, it was *something* she saw. I said, "A *deer*."
"No." "Waal, you know, they put that white *tail* up..."

Morris: ...uh-huh...

James: She says, "No, No. It wasn't a *deer*." (*Pause.*) It was a *boy*." She said she *felt* something, you know, like you do...

Morris: Mm...

James: ...she looked *around*...

Morris: Where was she?

James: On the porch...

Morris: Mm.

James: There was a *boy*. He *saw* her, and he ran up the lane. (*Pause.*) Now: (*Pause.*) Where would he be *coming* from ... ?

Morris: ... I don't know.

James: Well, I don't know *either*. Nothing up there, and what would he be *doing* up there ... ? (*Pause.*)

Morris: Now when was this?

James: Just at dusk. I said, "You see funny things in that light." (*Pause.*) "Yes," she says, "I saw this plain as day, though, and it was a *boy*. He *saw* me, and he ran away."

Morris: Did she say what he was wearing?

James: No, and I'll tell you, I didn't want to *press* her. (*Pause.*)

Morris: Uh-huh.

James: ... cause she was growing frightened. (*Pause.*)

Morris: She'd *seen* something.

James: Mm.

Morris: You know what it was?

James: No, I don't. (*Pause.*) No.

Morris: Mm.

James: I know there's places in the woods where I don't like to *go* ...

Morris: Mm. (*Pause.*) There's places I don't like to go *either*. (*Pause.*)

James: *You* don't ...

Morris: (*Pause.*) No. (*Pause.*)

James: Mm.

A: ... don't have the twelve-inch. We have the ten-inch and the fourteen-inch.

B: Isn't that always the way?

A: Seems it is. A number two do?

B: No.

A: Alright. The guy should have been in *Tuesday*, I spect him *Friday*, if he don't come then ... I'll tell you, I've been thinking of switching. 'Merican *United*, I can get twenty percent over a year, you sign on to their Ownership Subscriber Plan, you get a basis of twenty percent, you want something it's *there*. The next day. Six days.

B: Where they out of?

A: Down in Manchester. *Basis* of twenty percent, they've got a *newspaper*, what do you call it, a *flyer*, the *specials*, they can go, sometimes they beat the Marketway sixty percent.

B: No.

A: Absolutely.

B: How's the quality?

A: Same, better. Most things better, much of ... what they *do*. *You* know, they've got their *brand* ...

B: Uh huh ...

A: *Good* stuff. Heavy gauge stuff. Some of ... *you* know their stuff ...

B: ... sure ...

A: ... same patterns eighteen ninety-eight ...

B: When's that, when they got started?

A: When they got started. Yes. Fellow name of ... I had the guy in here, I was looking at their stuff since I came in. You have to sign *up*, what you do, you buy stock in the *company*, the minimum buy-in thirty-two hundred dollars, you own *stock*, at the end of the year they go and pro*rate* you the amount of your sales, and you're discounted based on that.

B: And what do you do with the discount?

A: What do you do?

B: What, do you apply it to your...

A: Well, I guess you do. I never thought of it. I suppose that you... or you could take it in cash. I had the guy here just the other day.

B: They want you to sign up.

A: The closest, *Jims*, in *Brandenburgs* American...

B: He is...?

A: Oh yeah. You see his prices in there? Beat the *Marketway* fifteen percent *easily*. On *everything*. He *has* to...

B: They spend their money on advertising.

A: That's what I'm *saying*. It ain't going in the *stock*, in stock improvement...dealer *relations*...it's going in the *television* ads. Schiff, started eighteen ninety-eight. American United, the whole operation's built on one thing: the relation with the *dealer*.

B: Mm.

A: Stockholders are the dealer, *customers* the dealer. Everything. Geared toward one man. I pick up the phone, I say, "Where are the... *whatever*, he said that they'd be here on *Thursday*. Marketway, what do *they* care...? No *displays*, very few *incentives*...like I'm buying *retail* from them. You complain to someone, their attitude, basically, I think, I don't think they do it on *purpose*, but what you get is: if you don't want the franchise, you can turn back. They don't care. What they think, they're doing you a *favor*, all the money they've spent on the TV ads. Some stores, maybe, though I doubt it. Not in *here*. A fella comes in here he wants three of those, four of those, something he broke on a job, he wants it this afternoon: *I'm* built on *service*. He goes down the road, he can go to the *Star* supply in *Worth*, he's in the habit to come here, I want to *keep* him here. Two things they told me: Never change your hours, never cut your stock.

B: Uh-huh.

A: A fellow comes by some hour you're spose to be open and you're *closed*, next time he thinks heavily fore he drives out of his way. "Maybe he's closed..."

B: That's very true.

A: ...it makes no difference it only happened one time. It's like adultery. I'm not foolin you. He thinks, "It happened once, it could happen again."

B: Uh-huh.

A: Fellow comes in here something he needs on a job, he needs it this afternoon, I'm *out* of it, what does he think? "*Shit*, I could of drove the same distance to *Star* and had it, and probably *cheaper*..." Something else: If I can get with the *American* I'm going to beat Marketway, I'm going to beat *Star*. I'm going to have them coming *here* from Worth...

B: You think?

A: There's no two ways about it. I'll have the variety, I'll have *quality*.... They marshal their *franchises very* careful. Forty-two miles to Brandenburgs, the closest they could have another is here. I've got no competition. I'll have them coming in from Worth, from *Peacham*...

B: And it's just the down payment...

A: What it is, yes, it's a down payment, it's an *investment*, you're actually buying stock. Whatever it is, I looked it up a week ago, a couple of weeks ago, seventeen dollars a share. What is that? Two into thirty-five, two shares for thirty-five, two hundred shares, thirty-five hundred dollars. Which you earn the dividend on, too, whatever that is...

B: On the stock.

A: Yes.

B: You should go with them.

A: I *would.* I *would* and I think I will. I think June and I have almost decided to *go* with them. It's a big step, but I think it's worth it. That's what I think. Many things. You have to look down the road. It's a big step now, it's a big *investment*, it's a *commitment*, in certain ways it would mean taking on more *stock....*

B: Why is that?

A: Well, you have a basic *order.* Whatever your *size* is: the classification that they give you...on your *footage*...on your *overhead*...then when you order you have a minimum order that you have to file. (*Pause.*) You also have a minimum order per *month*...they come in and they do the inventory...

B: *They* do.

A: Yep. They do. At the end of the year...I think that that's a good idea. They come in, a team, ten people, something, calculators, they're out in an afternoon, they come in Sunday afternoon...whenever you're closed, they work through the night, they're out Monday morning. *That's* a good idea.... You ever do an inventory?

B: No.

A: Hell on Earth. I worked in a shoe store once. I thought I was going to go mad.... But it's a big step. (*Pause.*)

B: Mm.

A: (*Pause.*) It's a big step. (*Pause.*)

B: *Well—*

A: Yeaaah! Five of the Number three. Twelve-inch. I'm almost sure I'll have them Friday.

B: I'll be back.

A: I'm going to call him again today. I would say ninety percent. Ninety-five percent. I'll have them Friday. I'll tell you: If he *doesn't* come in, I'll pick them up, you stop in Saturday morning...

B: *That's* okay...

A: No. I should *have* 'em. No trouble at all. You come in Friday, he hasn't stopped in, I'll have 'em Saturday first thing.

B: That's alright.

A: No trouble at all. I'm sorry I don't *have* 'em. I *should*. It doesn't help *you* to tell you that the *man* didn't come in.

B: Well, *thank* you.

A: That's alright. You take care, now.

B: You, too.

A: It's nice talking to you.

DOWSING

Two older men, in a Vermont country store.

A: *Yessuh.* Fella told me he said, "I don't want no more of them *dowsers* in here." By garry, I said, he's got a thing or two to learn.

B: I *guess*...

A: I said to you, Jim, *you're* a Mason, I said you did something I don't like, "I don't want no more *Masons* in here..."

B: No. Mason's supposed t'believe in brotherhood.

A: Yes. But if I told *you* something you did, I'se going to, you know, take it *out* on...

B: Yuh.

A: ...on other *Masons*...

B: Well, I'd say that's *foolish.*

A: ...What *I'd* say.

B: You say he didn't want the *dowsers?*

A: *Dowsers* were down to his place...

B: ...uh-huh...

A: Some woman called, she wanted to know was her *friend* there, he says, "She's your friend, you should *know* if she's here." She called the chamber of *commerce*, he gets the *complaint*, the fella calls him up he says, "By garry, *keep* 'em!" says he'll do without 'em. Big mistake. One week of the year that they're here, he's *booked*, you know, they come to spend their *money*...

B: Uh-huh...

A: *They* don't care it cost twenty-five dollars, thirty-five, they don't care, they're, you know...

B: Um hmm...

A: Well, they're on *vacation. Any* business you meet some you'd rather not *deal* with. I think he's a *fool.*

B: Now: (*Pause.*) When you say "dowsin'"—is that the same dowsin' that we use to do with a bent stick?

A: It is.

B: For *water.*

A: Well, they dowse for *water,* dowse for *oil...*

B: For *oil...* ?

A: For oil in the ground. Yessuh.

B: ...that a fact...

A: It is. For... well, you know, they might, say, you know, if they wanted to lay out a *field,* what to put where...

B: ...yuh...

A: ...in what corner of the *field...*

B: Uh-huh...

A: They'd dowse for that.

B: And how'd they find it?

A: Little *string,* a *weight* on it, they dowse it, yes or no. (*Pause.*) Eh? They ask the *question,* string moves *one* way, then it's "yes." The other way is "no."

B: The way it *rotates.*

A: *Yessir.*

B: You know, I could never... fellas take that *stick...* you know, I took it, never did a thing, just laid there in my hand. Other man took it, twisted every *which* way...

A: I know.

B: Never did a *thing* for me.

A: Me, either. (*Pause.*)

B: And that is their *convention.* Is that the thing?

A: Yup. Up *Morristown. You* know that.

B: Yup.

A: Yuh.

B: Up to *Morristown.*

A: Yuh. (*Pause.*)

B: I heard it's going to frost tonight.

A: They had a fellow, Connie *Barr*...

B: Yuh.

A: You remember Connie?

B: Yes, I do.

A: His sister lost her watch, he found it with a dowsing stick.

B: Who was his sister?

A: Eunice Craft.

B: The *Craft* girls...?

A: No. She married Billy Craft.

B: She *married* Billy.

A: Yessir.

B: D'I know her?

A: I think you did.

B: Mm.

A: Lost her watch, he found it.

B: With a dowsing stick?

A: Uh-huh.

B: Where was it?

A: In the field.

B: In plain sight?

A: I don't *think* so. Cause she'd lost it for a month.

B: She had?

A: Yeh.

B: And he found it?

A: Yes. He did.

B: Most like he *put* it there.

A: Well, that's what we thought at the *time*, but he held out he found it dowsing.

B: How about that now.

A: And I think that he *did*.

B: Well, you know, the things that you *see*, it makes you think that maybe there's something to *everything*.

A: Now, by God, that's the truth.

B: Mm?

A: *Yessir.*

B: *Ayuh.*

DEER DOGS

Two men, Larry *and* Bunchy, *at a country store. There are also a couple of onlookers.*

Larry: Dog's runnin deer it should be shot.

Bunchy: But who's to tell it's runnin deer?

Law says you see a dog in pursuit of a deer you can *shoot* him. Who's to say it's...wait, wait, you take *Dave* here: Keeps his dog tied up. One day th' dog, say Larry *Thompson's* dog, is runnin by—*Dave's* dog gets loose... Larry's dog runnin deer. Someone sees it and, down the road later on, Larry's dog *and* Dave's dog. What does he do? Shoot'em both.

Larry: How did Dave's dog get loose?

Bunchy: ...I'm saying a dog which is *usually* tied down, *Dave's* dog...

Larry: How did it get loose?

Bunchy: I'm saying one day when it *is* loose...I don't *know* how it got loose...

Larry: And was it runnin deer...?

Bunchy: No.

Larry: How do you know?

Bunchy: Cause it hasn't got a *taste* for them. It's a tame dog.

Larry: How do you know?

Bunchy: Well, now, now, now, because it *is* a tame dog: I, you *know* that dog...

Larry: ...I'm...

Bunchy: ...*I* know what you're...

Larry: I'm...

Bunchy: I know what you're, wait a second—I know what you're saying...that the dog is, *though* the dog is tame, it gets loose it starts runnin deer. Is that it?

Larry: Yes.

Bunchy: But what I'm saying, this case we *know* that the dog is tame. It's *tame*. It *isn't* runnin deer. Alright? It's DAVE'S DOG. It's *tame*. It's been tied up constantly...

Larry: How does it...

Bunchy: ...that's not...

Larry: ...how does it get loose?

Bunchy: Well, say that Dave forgot to tie it up.

Larry: And where does it go?

Bunchy: ...I...

Larry: Where does it go?

Bunchy: I know what you're saying. It goes to the woods. Alright.

Larry: What is it doing there?

Bunchy: It's *out*. With Larry Thompson's dog.

Larry: What are they doing?

Bunchy: *Larry's* dog is runnin deer.

Larry: And what is Dave's dog doing?

Bunchy: I don't know.

Larry: Well, I don't know *either*—but *I'm* going to assume it's runnin deer. (*Pause.*)

Bunchy: Would you shoot it?

Larry: Yes, I would.

Bunchy: You'd shoot Dave's dog.

Larry: Yes. I would. (*Pause.*)

Bunchy: (*Snorts.*) You would shoot Dave's dog. (*Pause.*)

Larry: Yes. I would.

Bunchy: Because you know that *that's* the dog that'll be caught. Not Larry *Thompson's* dog. (*Pause.*) *That's* the dog that will be caught...*Shoot*. It's a bad law...I'm sorry. (*Pause.*) I don't like it.

Larry: You'll like it when you go out in the woods there ain't no *deer*...

Bunchy: (*Pause.*) *Nossir.* (*Pause.*) No *sir*...N' I'm going to tell you one more thing: What the *Law*...wait a second— what the law *encourages* a fella to do is—I'm not saying *you* or *me*, but what it sets a man up to do is to say, "I'm going to shoot that fella's *dog*." That's not right. (*Pause.*)

IN THE MALL

Scene: *a bench in a shopping mall.*
Characters: *A, a sixty-year-old man. B,
a thirteen-year-old boy.*

B: I bet I know where you got that ice cream cone.

A: Where?

B: Down the mall.

A: That's right.

B: What did you pay for it?

A: Eighty-five cents.

B: Eighty-five cents...

A: That's right.

B: Is that with the tax?

A: No.

B: What is it with the tax?

A: Eighty-nine.

B: Eighty-nine. That's right. I bought one there. (*Pause.*) I bought one there yesterday. What kind is it?

A: What kind is it?

B: Yes.

A: Butternut.

B: Butternut. I had one. (*Pause.*) They made it up. They made it up I went down there the guys in there, you know, down the mall, I don't know, they want everything just like they like it, you know what I mean? I went in there my shirt off, this guy he says, "Get out." (*Pause.*) I had to go. He was bigger than me—I would of wanted to smash his face in. Lots of people in there. They got a sign: "No Shoes, No Shirt, No Service," all they care, who they *like*. Somebody they *like* goes in there they give 'em anything he wants. I bought these crackers in a store they were crushed I took 'em back the guy said, "You ate some of 'em." I said I opened the box and I had a couple. "Eat the rest," he said. I knew a fella had a dog he fed it scraps. Whatever he didn't want to eat. When he had his dinner. They got that same hat down there. Where did you get that hat? (*Pause.*) Where did you get that hat? Down there?

A: No.

B: Where did you get it?

A: I bought it on a trip.

B: They've got the same one down there. I like to know that. I saw a picture of this guy in there he looked like somebody I know. (*Pause.*) You think it's cold here?

A: No.

B: You don't?

A: No. (*Long pause.*)

B: Do you think it's warm? (*Pause.*)

A: No.

B: Well, if you don't think it's cold and it's not warm what is it? (*Pause.*) What *is* it?

A: What is it here?

B: *Yeah. Huh???* I don't think it's cold. I don't *care* if it's cold. *Anyway.* I like to do things, you know, that people say that they can't do. I climbed this fence once that everyone said you can't get over. It had barb wire at the top. They make this stuff it's razors. It's a razor-ribbon you can't climb it. I went up. You hold on to the barb wire you go right over I came down on the other side. *They* didn't care. They said that it was stupid. I bought a pair of socks once they had stripes on top I folded 'em down. I thought, "Maybe this is to show us where to fold."

(A *gets up.*)

Where are you going?

A: Home.

B: Why?

A: Why?

B: Yeah.

A: Because I'm finished here.

B: You're finished doing what?

A: Sitting here.

B: You are?

A: Yes.

B: Do you have any money? (*Pause.*) I need some cause I've got to do things.

A: No. I don't have any.

B: You don't.

A: No.

B: Mm. Mm. Mm. Mm. (*Pause.*) Do you throw that thing away when you're done?

A: Yes.

B: Mm. Where?

A: In the wastebasket.

B: Mm. (*Pause.*) Mm. (*A exits.*) (*Pause.*) I had one one time...

MAPLE SUGARING

The sugar shack had light slanted through the vent in the roof, and white smoke billowed up.

Morris's father built the place in 1912, and Morris was stoking the fire up now with hardwood logs.

The sap was clearer than clean water and ran through the vat. There was a superfine white foam on it, and often Morris took a scoop and dipped it in the vat then let it drip to see the thickness of the sap.

His wife had made lunch. There was Canadian beer and Swiss cheese, hamburgers and cookies made with the syrup that we made yesterday. The coffee pot leaned up against the vat to keep it warm.

Everyone spoke in hushed tones. Susan had brought down her eight-month-old baby, and its grandmother, Morris's wife, set up Susan's old crib in the sugar shack.

He was asleep in the crib, and his grandmother was looking down at him. She said, "You're not the first child to nap in that crib while we were sugaring."

Later in the woods Joe, Susan, and I were carrying the sap in pails, and she carried the baby on her back, and when we stopped to rest she nursed the child.

By four o'clock my neck hurt and I was becoming dizzy. The day had turned cold, and the sap had ceased to run. Susan went in to set up dinner, I was left with Joe. We gathered the last buckets, and I longed to go to sleep.

In the sugar shack the benches were made of wood. There was a square door on a running track to the woodshed. The sun streamed through the large vent in the roof. The people talked in whispers. The steam rose. Joe's baby was asleep.

MORRIS AND JOE

Morris said, "Joe, 'member when we saw the bear in the tree?"

Joe smiled. "Remember when the milk froze?"

They were sitting on the step. The step had been removed from the house so they could repair the sill. It was an old house and the roof had leaked; the water ran down the post and rotted the sill. When they started the job Joe poked his pocketknife into it. It went in all the way.

The step was granite. Five-by-three. The bulldozer moved it back from the house. One corner was chipped out where there had been a bootscraper. Some hunters broke it out the year before.

Morris said, "You were shakin', Joe."

Joe said, "I wasn't shakin'. I was scared for *you*."

"You *were*?"

"Yes. I know how *skit*tish you get in moments of stress."

"*Aha*."

Joe passed his lunchbucket to Morris who took a doughnut from it.

They looked out at the woods.

"I wonder where he is," Morris said.

"Probably up to Canada," Joe said.

"You think so?"

"Yes."

"Scared him within an inch of his life," Morris said. "Uh-*huh* ..." Joe got up off the step.

"Where are you goin'?"

"I'm goin' to pee." Joe walked behind a stack of lumber. Morris said, "Yes*sir*, I hope he's back to Canada!"

"And why is that?" Joe said.

"'Cause he comes down here once again he better shake with *fear*. 'Cause he knows in America—he threatens our estates—there's not a man jack isn't ready to shoot himself in the foot."

"Do you remember when the milk froze?" Joe said.

"*Yes*sir. Smack in the foot," Morris said.

"*Susan* reminded me of that," Joe said. "That time that Morris cleaned the tank out." Joe came back buttoning up his fly. "How lovely all the driveway looked covered in milk..."

"You want some coffee?" Morris said.

"...and how proud we were to defend you," Joe said, "from all that pernicious talk that you were drunk."

"People can sure be thoughtless," Morris said.

"That is the truth."

"Take you and that *bear*, frinstance," Morris said. "No mercy to dumb animals; just a display of wrath, and one man hopping with a .22 Long in his foot."

"I only hit the boot," Joe said.

"You want another cup of coffee?"

"No thanks."

Morris stretched and stood up. He closed his lunchpail. "*Yes*sir!"

"You want me to go back to those left joists this afternoon?" Joe said.

"How many more you got to do?"

"Just the two."

"Might as well go do 'em."

They stood for a moment and looked at the sky. Joe sighed. "He sure was pretty singing in that tree."

"Yes. He was," Morris said.

"Where do you think he is today?"

"I'm sure he's back in Canada."

Morris spat on the ground. "Yup," he said.

"Yessir," Joe said. They went back into the house.

The Dog

The Dog, Film Crew, and *Four A.M.* were first presented at Jason's Park Royal in New York as part of the Three by Three program on July 14, 1983, with the following cast directed by Joe Cacaci:

The Dog	*Film Crew*	*Four A.M.*
John Savoia	Brian Smiar	Bill Cwikowski
	John Savoia	Michael Wikes

Talk about a dog! Talk about a precious animal! A little fluffball. A furry little nothing. But ballsy as a paratrooper.

He's tough, but I'm *tougher*. Benjy may be tough but I'm yet tougher.

Go after dogs twice his size. Three, four times his size. Go right up to 'em. Sniff 'em. Smell 'em up and down...

He growls, bares his teeth.

He scares 'em. He's little, but goddamn it if he's not a scrapper. And they know it. Damn right they do, too.

Sensitive?

He's more sensitive than most *people*. Makes most people look sick, he's so sensitive. In tune like a human.

He picks up on things, too.

I come home, he meets me at the door. Grinning, breathing fast, he's glad to see me.

I go to hang up my coat, and what do I find? The little pisser has shit on the floor! He's crossed me. My best friend has crossed me.

So I go over to him, he's grinning like a sonofabitch, and I say *sit*. And he sits down and cocks his head, wondering what's up.

I make a fist, and lean over and whack the shit outta him. He goes clear across the room and just lays there on his side.

So then I say *get up* and he gets up. And I say *sit* and he sits down again and I walk over to him.

So he's purebred, he's no dummy. And he figures maybe I'm going to knock him around again, and he's a little scared.

But he hangs right in there.

I say *stay*. And it's like he's glued to the floor. He'd sit there for a year if I didn't tell him different.

So I go over and get a chair and bring it back and put it right in front of him. I sit down, lean back, and cross my legs.

I look at him. He looks at me.

After a minute or so, I lean forward and say, very reasonable and soft, I say "Don't shit on the floor. Now, get outta here."

And I never have to say a word on the subject again.

Film Crew

Two men: Joe *and* Mike

Joe: Did you make this up?

Mike: No. I mean, you know, I *embellished* it. Yeah. I made part of it up.

Joe: Uh-huh.

Mike: The nice thing, you know, I guess I've taught it to, say ten or fifteen crews...

Joe: Uh-huh.

Mike: ...over the last four years, the *nice* thing, I'll be out somewhere, someone will say, "I'll teach you this...," and I can trace it back. "Where did you *learn* it from...?" and I can trace it back to, you know...

Joe: Yeah...

Mike: To someone who I taught. (*Pause.*) And, you know, you play *tournaments*...and you can play for *money*...

Joe: How?

Mike: You play *points*.

Joe: Oh. Yeah.

Mike: Sure. And what you have left in your hand is what you're stuck with.

Joe: Whoever goes *out*.

Mike: Yeah. If you're stuck with fifteen *points*...

Joe: Uh-huh...

Mike: And you can play, you know, a *dime* a point, *penny* a point...

Joe: ...yeah.

Mike: ...*buck* a point. You get stuck with an *ace* in your hand, that's fifteen bucks right there.

Joe: Right.

Mike: One night on my last shoot...?

Joe: Uh-huh?

Mike: Night shoot?

Joe: Yeah?

Mike: To get to sleep, we musta played, six, seven games. (*Pause.*) We were up, Jesus, till noon. I won a hundren twenty bucks.

Joe: Yeah?

Mike: *Oh* yeah. Oh yeah. *Easily.* (*Pause.*)

Joe: Now, what's this thing with jacks?

Mike: It's simple: If you play a jack, then you must cover it. (*Pause.*)

Joe: Uh-huh.

Mike: With another card. (*Pause.*)

Joe: "Cover" it. (*Pause.*)

Mike: Play another card on top of it.

Joe: Right.

Mike: Of the same suit.

Joe: Right.

Mike: Or denomination.

Joe: Right. And if you can't?

Mike: You have to draw another card. *But!* But, of course, if you have more than one jack in your hand, then you can play *that* jack on it. (*Pause.*)

Joe: Uh-huh.

Mike: So, you'd play your jack, you have to *cover* it. (*Pause.*) Are you with me?

Joe: Yes.

Mike: Alright. You cover it with another jack, and then you have to cover it again.

Joe: Again?

Mike: Of course. Because you've played a jack.

Joe: Right. Alright.

Mike: You see?

Joe: Yes.

Mike: It's still a jack.

Joe: Yes. Right.

Mike: And you can play as many jacks as you've got in your hand, with, of course, with two decks, that's eight jacks. If you have them in your hand.

Joe: And you cover the last card.

Mike: Yes. Now. Now: For each jack you play, you skip one man. (*Pause.*)

Joe: Uh-huh.

Mike: So: you play your jack, you skip the man to your ri— left; second jack, two, men. Et cetera.

Joe: Right.

Mike: It's simple.

Joe: And the last card that you cover must be the same suit.

Mike: Right. Just like any other card. (*Pause.*) Or denomination.

Joe: Right. Except that that would be a jack.

Mike: Right. Right. I'm sorry. Or an eight. (*Pause.*)

Joe: What's this thing with fours?

Mike: Fours. Very simple. When you play a *four*...when you play a *four*...?

Joe: Yes?

Mike: The direction of play changes. (*Pause.*) Right?

Joe: Right. (*Pause.*)

Mike: It's very simple: Man on your right plays, *you* play. You play a four, it goes right back to him. Now *he* must play again. (*Pause.*) You see?

Joe: Yes. And then the man on *his* right.

Mike: Yes. (*Pause.*) You must change the *direction*.

Joe: Right.

Mike: Good. (*Pause.*) That's it. Other than that it's regular.

Joe: How do you score?

Mike: Aces are *fifteen*...

Joe: ...yes...

Mike: Face cards are *ten*...

Joe: Uh-huh.

Mike: And every other thing is what it is. (*Pause.*) Okay?

Joe: Yes.

Mike: Wait. (*Pause.*) You know about the queen of spades?

Joe: No.

Mike: Queen of spades, the next man takes five cards. (*Pause.*) If you play the queen of spades, the next man must take five cards.

Joe: From the stack.

Mike: Yes. (*Pause.*) *Unless* he plays the queen of spades right back at you.

Joe: Can he do that?

Mike: Of course. There's two, right?

Joe: Right.

Mike: And that's the game. You want to try a practice hand? Wait! Wait: This is an important rule. Now: When you have ...wait. When you've played all of your cards but one *card* ...huh?

Joe: ...yes?

Mike: When you have only one card left to play, then you say, "Last Card."

Joe: "Last Card."

Mike: You must announce: "Last Card." If you *fail* you must take ten cards from the stack. (*Pause.*) You must say "Last Card" *before* the next man on your left plays. Or wherever. Before the next man plays. This is important, because *sometimes* you'll have one card and you'll forget to announce, so there's two guys on the far side, right, sitting over here, and you can call it any time until the next man plays, and *save* yourself, so we're here waiting for the next guy to *play*, right? And you can call it any time. So we're avoiding your *eyes* ...

Joe: Right...

Mike: And trying not to call *attention* ... so that he will play, and we can call it on you. Before you remember. (*Pause.*) Ha.

Joe: Does that happen very often?

Mike: Oh. Oftener than you might think. *Oh* yeah.

Joe: Mm.

Mike: *Oh* yeah. (*Pause.*) And that's the game. (*Pause.*) That's it. Do you want to try a practice hand?

Four A.M.

An announcer seated at a radio studio console desk. He wears earphones and speaks into a microphone. We hear the voice of the caller over a loudspeaker.

Interviewer: Hello, you're on the air.

Caller: Hello, Greg, how are you?

Int: I'm fine.

Caller: Good. Greg, it's a pleasure to talk with you. I had the pleasure of talking to you three-and-one-half *years* ago, and I've been a continual listener of yours since you started out with the twenty-two stations, and I admire you very much.

Int: Thank you.

Caller: Thank *you*, Greg.

Int: What's your problem?

Caller: Greg, we need your help to publicize our plan. We've been trying to get our organization together to raise money to be able to hire a public relations firm like Wells and Jacoby to publicize our organization. (*Pause.*) Where are we going to *get* the money...? *I* don't know...

Int: To publicize your...

Caller: In the movie *2001*, based on the writings of Arnold Toynbee, they speak of the plan...

Int: Excuse me, excuse me, but the movie *2001* was based on the writings...

Caller: ...all human life is made of molecules...

Int: ...based on the writings of Arthur C. Clarke...

Caller: All human...no, Greg, if you examine...

Int: ...it was based on the writings of Arthur C. Clarke...

Caller: Oh, Greg, *No*. We have the...

Int: Well, go on.

Caller: ...we have the writings.

Int: Okay, go on.

Caller: *Greg:* In the writings of Arnold Toynbee he discusses a plan whereby all human life could be easily re-constituted on the planet Jupiter.

Int: Uh-huh...(*Pause.*)

Caller: Greg?

Int: Yes? (*Pause.*) I'm listening.

Caller: Greg...

Int: Yes?

Caller: In the wr...

Int: Yeah. I got it. Go on.

Caller: In the...

Int: No, no. No. Go *on*. I *got* it. Arnold Toynbee, human life on...

Caller: As we're made of molecules, Greg, and the *atoms* of all human life that ever lived are still in all of us...

Int: Okay, I got it. They exist, they've just been rearranged. (*Pause.*)

Caller: Yes. (*Pause.*)

Int: *So*?

Caller: We'd like to publicize our organization, Greg. We're very young. We've just been in existence over a year and we want to *publicize* our theory. And, Greg, we don't know *how*.

Int: You...how do you publicize your plan to bring dead people back to life on *Jupiter*.

Caller: Yes.

Int: *Why*? (*Pause.*) Why would you want to do this? (*Pause.*) Hello?

Caller: Yes?

Int: Why would you want to *do* this? (*Pause.*) You see what I'm saying to you? (*Pause.*) What is the aim of your group?

Caller: Greg...

Int: What are your *plans*? (*Pause.*)

Caller: I ... (*Pause.*)

Int: *What?*

Caller: I ... Greg, I *told* you.

Int: You said that you want to bring dead people back to life.

Caller: Yes.

Int: On the planet Jupiter.

Caller: Just as they showed us in the mo...

Int: Well, I'm not sure that's what the movie was about, but be that as it may, why would you want to do that?

Caller: Oh, Greg, you can't *mean* it...

Int: Well, *yes*, I mean it. Why would you ... what's the idea ...? You're walking down the street, there's Abraham *Lincoln* ... is that the idea?

Caller: Yes.

Int: ... so anybody that you want to *talk* to, so forth, there they are. Is that the idea? (*Pause.*)

Caller: Yes.

Int: Who do you *pick?* Who *picks* 'em?
   You? Your organization? ... or do you just bring 'em *all* back? (*Pause.*) What is your ... I mean, do you have a *program* for this? Or ... what are your *goals* ...? (*Pause.*)

Caller: To bring...

Int: Naah ... it's too *broad.* It's too *broad.* Don't you *see* what I'm talking about? You can't bring 'em *all* back. (*Pause.*) *Can* you?

Caller: I don't know.

Int: Well, *think* about it. (*Pause.*) *Think* about it.
   You're talking about billions of people. Eh?
   They've *lived* at different times. They speak different *languages*—the ones that speak our language, it's *changed* over the years. The *dialects* are different. *Customs* change. Their *lives* are different. Some of them died violent *deaths*

...some are *disfigured*...they've been *decomposing*....Now: listen to *this:* At what point do you bring them *back*? (*Pause.*) Right before they *died*? What if they were *ill*? What if they were *infirm*? And so you don't do it then, when *do* you do it? At what point? You see what I'm telling you? Someone wants to come back at age *twenty*, so you bring him back at fifty- five...is he allowed to *change*? And who's to say if he can or he can't? What if he never wanted to come back?

Caller:...Greg...?

Int: What about people who *killed* themselves. Because they didn't want to live? Some of them we know. We could leave *out*. What about ones that we *don't* know? Who's going to pass on this? You and your *group*? Well, then you're talk- ing about something very much like fascism. Is that what you want? Because I'll tell you what you get very quickly is a State where only the *Pure* can come back. Or the *good- looking*...or whatever the people in charge that day seem to feel is the ultimate good...and tickles their fancy. Or do you just press a button and *everyone* comes back? And what do you have then? I'll *tell* you what you have: *wars*. You've got wars. Unless you think that that being dead *improved* them. You see what I'm saying? You've got the same *jeal- ousies* and...misunder*stand*ings you had the *first* time. And how do you explain the technology to some guy who's just come back from 1565 and all of a sudden he's in some *space* suit and he's *alive* again...

Caller: He wouldn't be in a space suit.

Int:...whatever. And who *governs* this august group? Or do they just "get along"? Not in *this* lifetime, friend. What do you think? Because they're on a foreign planet that it's going to be cooperation and good *will*? They're going to forget about their human nature and just live in joy? You're talking about *heaven*, my friend. Heaven doesn't exist. You think the fact that they've come back is going to make them all philosophers? I don't think so. For a *day, yes*. *Maybe*. A week, a month later, and I'm going to tell you something: It's going to be worse than it was before, and you know what you've got? Chaos. And any time you get a *State* like that you have a populace that thinks the world owes it a living. And you've got a tragedy. It doesn't hold up. Even as a dream. It's not thought out. And what do they eat?

Caller: Toynbee says we can bombard the atmosphere with oxygen and reclaim the soil.

Int: *Does* he? And what if he's *wrong*...? (*Pause.*) You see what I'm saying? (*Pause.*)

Caller: I...

Int: You see what I'm telling you?

Caller: I...

Int: Listen to me: The world is full of histories of people trying to live in *Utopias*. It doesn't work. We wish it *did*, it *doesn't*. (*Pause.*) Alright? (*Pause.*) Alright?

Caller: Um...yes.

Int: *Alright*. Thank you for calling. (*Loudspeaker goes dead.*) Let's move along:

The Power Outage

The Power Outage was first published in the *New York Times* on August 6, 1977.

1: The thing which I'm telling you is no one enjoys being equal.

2: Yes. Yes. I agree with that. We have our fictions. And what did you do when the lights went out?

1: Stumbled around in the dark. (*Sotto voce.*)...taking goods away...they took the goods away. (*Full voice.*) Goods cannot take away heat.

2: No.

1: As if, if they were stolen, they could take the dark away.

2: No. I agree with you.

1: A flashlight runs on batteries, as does a candle, if you follow me.

2 (*Sotto voce*): No.

1: But here we find electric light has a *connection*.

2: Yes. I see your point. Yes.

1: Like a road, eh?

2: Yes.

1: It is the same road. One for all. A dirt path in the Hinterlands, of some worn blacktop in the Ozarks. It is all the same. One road.

2 (*Sotto voce*): One road.

1: Now we see the same of electricity. Why do we need these things?

2: The goods?

1: Yes. (*Pause.*)

2: They keep us cool.

1: Oh. (*Sighs.*) I tell you. It's like being at the Y.

2: The Blackout?

1: Yes. When you have taken off your clothes and they cannot see where you bought your watch.

2 (*Sotto voce*): Mmm.

1: When they turned the power off. So when the men were in the streets all bets were off.

2 (*Sotto voce*): When they went after goods. I know. It says they put them forty to a room too small for ten.

1: They did?

2: I read they did.

1: When they had caught them.

2: Yes.

1: You know, when you go in a record store you see the men with guns.

2: I know.

1: In Medieval England we learn they had seven hundred crimes which they could hang you for. We see that, and we are aghast. But now, today, you see them in the Supermarkets with their guns. They are empowered to kill you for the theft of record albums. (*Pause.*) Of some diversionary device or machine.

2 (*To self*): And they were very hot in there.

1: So when the men were in the streets, they said all bets are off. "You cannot live in Darkness. You insure your power by the gun." (*Pause.*) What audacity.

2: I think so, too.

1: Today you cannot buy a flashlight.

2: It is difficult, but you can buy them.

1: Do you know, the folks directing traffic...

2: Yes.

1: Controlling traffic in their nightdress, as in Revolutionary Times. This is not altruism.

2: No. We'd all like to direct it.

1: It is wish-fulfillment.

2 (*To self*): Until they came to Trial...

1: Or they would go destroy a mercantile concern.

2 (*To self, continuing*): which would not be soon...

1: And cause much unhappiness. (*Pause.*)

2: Someone should write a book.

1: There. In the dark. Our dreams of courage, or The Indians. Of foraging.

2: We all revert.

1: You think so?

2: Yes.

Food

Two men: C *and* D

C: I've loved eating and I've *always* loved eating. My *father* died of insulin shock. The day they put him in the hospital his blood pressure was twenty over eighty, wanted to dose him with *insulin*, he told them "no." They *killed* him. He, one time, had a saccharin reaction, in the fifties, when they took it, when it was in everything. He proved their case. (*Pause.*) He was the one, the cases of his type, why it's no longer *in*... in *sodas*... (*Pause.*) in *food*...

D: You're saying that it was his case?

C: Yes.

D: In what way, you're saying he took them to court?

C: Not in that sense, no. Cases of his type. You understand?

D: Yes.

C: (*Pause.*) And he overate. Those days... you know...

D: Yes.

C: You know how it was. *Later* we had no sugar in the house. You couldn't *find* it, for we didn't *have* it there. *Nothing.* And my mother was assiduous in cleansing it out; you remember, though, when we were young. It was in *everything.* The *cereal*... the *tea*... the *coffee*... *rolls*... you could go right through the day.... *Lunch*... (*Pause.*) My idea later of dessert was half a grapefruit, but *then* and you, too, I know. When we were young... the *oatmeal*...? My father put sugar on *fruit.*

D: My father, too.

C: My father put sugar on *water*melon.

D: My father did, too.

C: Looking back, he was a sick man. He was a very sick man. (*Pause.*) He must have been. All of the *effort* that he spent in balancing his diet; or, to say it on a different plane (because, finally, his diet did not admit of a balance), to achieve *rest*; he was trying to find *rest.* In himself. In food. For one moment. I think. In his life. Because of the *food* he ate. To overcome the *harm* that he had done, as I'm sure that he knew. The *milk* to overcome the sugar; the *caffeine* to overcome the cloying effect of the milk, which, I think, in the future, will be seen to be the worst. The worst of what we eat, for *all* that we say it is natural.

D: What?

C: Dairy.

D: Dairy products.

C: Yes. And *nicotine* to calm the harm that he did with caffeine. And *meat* to give him energy he needed. Not for "life." Not for his daily "life," but to combat the effects of the *food*. He, I saw him put butter on his *steak*...

D: I've seen that, too.

C: And *salt*. (*Pause.*) Salt on everything. Sugar and salt. We put sugar on *straw*berries... (*Pause.*)

D: What about your mother? (*Pause.*)

C: She... my mother... (*Pause.*)

D: Yes.

C: As a *cook*...

D: Yes.

C: How was she as a *cook*...?

D: Yes. (*Pause.*)

C: You know she died...

D: No. (*Pause.*)

C: She... she... (*Pause.*) She was the *cook*. (*Pause.*) She, uh, (Pause.) she cooked as she was *taught*. What else could she *do*? *Nothing*. What did *any* of us know? Nothing. "Eat Milk. It's Good for You!" And *alcohol*. Drink...? (*Pause.*) He drank all night. That's how I was brought up. You, too. No—I won't *touch* it now.

D: You don't touch drink?

C: I'll tell you what else: I don't miss it. Not one bit. The hardest I think was caffeine. Aaaaaand *salt*. Well, it's in everything. I used to drink club *soda*. No. You can't drink that. It's *salt*. That's all it is. That's why they *drink* it. You can't lie to yourself. Because if you do, your *body* will inform you. If you're lying to yourself. (*Pause.*) You see? (*Pause.*) As it starts to cleanse itself it will inform you. (*Pause.*) *Cigars.* You know me...

D: Yes.

C: Someone gave me one at *Thanksgiving*...

D: Mm.

C: An *Uppman.* I'd eaten too much. Eh? (*Pause.*) My body was *acid*, so I craved *nicotine.* And so I told myself: "Waaal, it's a *holiday*," as if it were a reward to poison my system ...So I smoked the cigar...(*Pause.*) I didn't even *want* it. While I smoked it I had to remind myself that it was a reward. I woke up in the night in *sweat.* My sweat stank of cigars. The *sheets* stank. When I washed them they still smelled. Your body's a machine. As trite as it is, it is true. If you don't change it today when are you going to change it? (*Pause.*) *Never.* He died as he wouldn't change. He knew more than they knew. They killed him anyway. *Why?* Because he was helpless. Because he was *ill.* Then he was at their mercy. And, I want to tell you, any time that that occurs your opponents will harm you. That's the nature of the world. Not *me.* Not *me.* My body is my friend. It does not want to do me ill. It does not want to be diseased. It is my friend. (*Pause.*) It is not my enemy. It killed my father. It will not kill *me.* It killed my *brother*—it will not kill *me.* It has killed *many.* It will not kill *me.* It is my *friend.* My body is my *friend.*

Columbus Avenue

Columbus Avenue was first published in the *Village Voice* on September 10, 1980.

I felt the cold steel of a gun against my head three times.

Twenty-six years we have been here. A tailor fourteen years before that here. Fifty-one years.

And he's an Orthodox Jew, and his father said (when he was managing: when first we settled on a price; and, you know, we *negotiated*...but when we were done he told me): "I will never throw you out."

The boy, he said, "Before I do a thing we'll talk." Today I get his letter in the mail. And I go there. I say, "You said that we were going to talk." He said, "I thought instead of talking I'd send you a letter."

So what am I going to do? Where am I going to go?

My customers are going to follow me? Can I ask them to walk for twenty blocks?

If even he gave me a *ten*-year lease, at least then I could sell the business.

So I said *double* the rent. *Triple* the rent, I told him.

He has got a *guy* is going to pay two thousand a month, he says. *And* he's going to put in fifty-thousand dollars restoration.

I told him, "How is he going to make the *rent*?"

He said, "He'll break his back. He'll break his back the first year," (he didn't say "back") "and, after that, he *fails*, I've got his fifty thousand he put in my building, and I rent the place again."

It's like that the whole street: Things you don't want at what you can't afford, and nothing that you need.

No services.

Where am I going to go?

If I was twenty, if I was even ten years *younger*...

Where am I going to go? I got to move the *press*, I got to move the *racks*; by the time I put *in* I put in all my savings to the *business* to go somewhere else and I have nothing. And I have to start again. Twenty-six years.

I told him, "I hate to remind you what your *father* said." He shrugged.

My *wife* went. I was getting sick. He said he'd give us an extension for six months.

It's the same all the neighborhood.

Let the depression come, and see who pays the rent.

Twenty-six years I've been here, and there are no more services on this street anymore.

What will people do I don't know what he thinks.

I don't know.

I don't know what I can say.

Steve McQueen

A monologue. The speaker is a man in his mid-to-late thirties.

...well, *I'm* from Hawaii—I met him when he was at the Kalona Mar, he was there two months.

He wasn't well. You know. We'd *talk*...we got to talking motorcycles. He asked if he could borrow my bike, I said of course. He got to taking it out every day. He was registered there as "McGuire." He was keeping a low profile, you know? But after a week or two, you know, I think that he was lonely. I'd see him around the pool. He must have seen me one morning coming to work on my bike, because he asked me about it: How was it *riding*, something; and we started talking about bikes. He had at that time over one hundred bikes in his collection...I don't know where they were...in the States.

You know, *The Great Escape*...? He did those stunts himself. You know where he jumps the barb wire? He did that himself—though it wasn't barb wire.

He found out that I was into martial arts and we took to sparring. He was in great shape—even though his disease—he was strong as a horse at that time. A fifty-sixty-minute workout was nothing to him. I'll tell you something else is he would drink a case of beer a day. Twenty-four beers a day. Lowenbrau. I know because I used to bring them to him. And smoke like a chimney. I guess he was just one of those men who are blessed with a completely perfect constitution. Though he was in great pain. I know that he was.

Indians...Harleys...Nortons...he had all of them. Did you know on the old *Indian* the oil used to go through the frame? It flowed through the frame.

You know the stunt on *The Great Escape* where they get the bike? The German motorcycle rider's coming down the road, they stretch a wire...? They had the greatest motorcycle rider in the world...*Rusty*, something...*Rusty*... they told him "Just drive down the road." They told him, "Be ready for anything." That's why it's so authentic. He runs into that wire...? He didn't know it was there. They did it in one take. (*Pause.*)

I met his son. (*Pause.*) At that time he was training as a flight instructor. I stayed at his house in Malibu. Three days.

Yes

Two men: A *and* B.

A: People don't know when they're well-off.

B: Now that's for sure.

A: That's for *goddamned*...what did you say? It *is* for sure. It's for god-*damned* sure. I swear to Christ. I swear on the grave of my mother, may she roast in peace...

B: What did you say? "May she roast in peace"?

A: Did I say what?

B: You said your mother.

A: Yes?

B: May she...(*Pause.*)

A: May she what? (*Pause.*)

B: She's dead, right?

A: Is she dead?

B: Is she?

A: Is that what you're asking me? (*Pause.*) Is my mother dead?

B: Am I asking you that?

A: Are you?

B: Well, is she dead? I *assume* that...she's *dead*, right?

A: (*Pause.*) Yes. (*Pause.*) *Yes.* She *is.*

B: (*Pause.*) I, um...

A: You're "sorry"?

B: I am sor...of, yes, of, ab...did she...of *course* I'm... did she...

A: Did she die recently?

B: Yes.

A: Recently? Peaceably...? I don't mean "peaceably," I mean *peacefully*...peacefully. Yes. Recently. Yes....I suppose they're the same thing. No...of course...of *course* they're not. They're not the...yes. She's *dead.* She's absolutely *dead.* How's *your* mom? Fine, I hope.

B: She's dead.

A: How about that?

B: I'm not glad that she's dead.

A: Well, that makes you a loyal *son, doesn't* it?

B: I liked her.

A: I'm very sure you did. That's "fine." That's truly "fine" of you. What was I saying? (*Pause.*) What was I speaking of, if I may?

B: You mentioned your mother.

A: Yes. I did. I said...what did I say? People are not well-off.

B: You said:

A: I spoke about my mother. *Thank* you.

B: ...something...

A: ...that's correct...

B: "My mother..."

A: "may she rest in hell" ra...ra...rrrra...raaa...rrrr... "may she..." "may she *rot* in hell" "may she..." (*Pause.*) What's the phrase? MAY SHE REST IN PEACE! What's the phrase?

B: May she rest in peace.

A: What's the phrase? (*Pause.*) What's the phrase for that? (*Pause.*)

B: That's it.

A: That's it?

B: Yes. (*Pause.*)

A: There's another one.

B: There is?

A: What is it?

B: I don't know.

A: ...the *phrase* for it...*you* know what I...(*Pause.*) I must be a deeply troubled man. (*Pause.*) So many things accept me.

B: What are they?

A: I mean *"accept"* me.

B: What did you say? (*Pause.*)

A: I said...(*Pause.*)

B: You said that you must be...

A: ...I said that things *accept* me.

B: What did you...?

A: I...

B: ...you said...(*Pause.*)

A: ...I...(*Pause.*)...I...(*Pause.*)...I...

THE BLUE HOUR: CITY SKETCHES

Prologue: American Twilight

Doctor

The Hat

Businessmen

Cold

Epilogue

The following pieces were written variously as curtain rais-
ers for other plays of mine, as cabaret pieces, and as experiments. They were written to be performed on a bare
stage, using only a chair or two, and without props or special
costuming.

The Blue Hour was first performed as a workshop at the
Public Theater in New York, in February, 1979 with the
following cast directed by David Mamet: Ben Halley, Jr.,
David Sabin, Arthur French, Patti LuPone, and Lindsay
Crouse.

Characters
Prologue: American Twilight: Man
Doctor: Doctor, Woman
The Hat: Customer, Saleswoman
Businessmen: Grey, Black
Cold: A, B
Epilogue: Man

PROLOGUE: AMERICAN TWILIGHT

Man: In great American cities at *l'heure bleu* airborne dust particles cause buildings to appear lightly outlined in black. The people hurry home. They take a taxi or they walk or crush into the elevated trains or subways; or they go into the library where it is open and sit down and read a magazine and wait a bit so that the crush of travelers will dissipate.

This is the Blue Hour.

The sky is blue and people feel blue.

When they look up they will see a light or "powder" blue is in the Western sky where, meanwhile, in the East the sky is midnight blue; and this shade creeps up to the zenith and beyond, and changes powder blue to midnight and, eventually, to black, whereat the buildings lose their outlines and become as stageflats in the glow of incandescent lamps. This is the Blue Hour—the American twilight as it falls today in the cities.

Doctor: Now, what seems to be your problem?

Woman: I won't pay this. (*Waves bill.*)

Doctor: Won't pay what, I'm sorry.

Woman: I won't pay this.

Doctor: Well, let's see what it is. (*Takes bill.*) Now, what's the problem here?

Woman: The problem is that it's outrageous. I had an appointment with you for four-thirty and you took me after six...

Doctor: Well, surely, you must realize...

Woman: No, no, I realize nothing of the sort. What makes you think that your time is more valuable, that my time is less valuable than yours? If you made an appointment you should keep to it.

Doctor (*Pause*): Mrs. Rudin, look.

Woman: No, you look. I'm alright. I'm fine, but people out there, there are worried people out there. Sitting, who knows *how* long, and you keep them there, they're waiting on your pleasure.

(*Pause.*)

Doctor: It isn't for my *pleasure*...

Woman: Then what is it for then?

Doctor: Mrs....

Woman: Eh...? Now what are two hours of *my* time worth? To you, obviously nothing.

Doctor: There are economic exigencies.

Woman: Are there?

Doctor: Yes, there are.

Woman: And what are they? (*Pause.*) What are they? That you think entitles you to treat people like cattle and then charge them like that?

Doctor: Mrs. Rudin, I am on call at three hospitals in New York, I maintain a complete...

Woman: That's your privilege. I didn't force you to do that. Those are *your* necessities. *Your* fiscal... I don't know. Why should I have to pay for that? (*Pause.*)

Doctor: Mrs. Rudin, what is your, now what is your complaint here?

Woman: I will not pay this bill. (*Pause.*)

Doctor: You won't.

Woman: I come here with a broken toe, I sit over three hours, and you take an x-ray and tell me my toe is broken. And you charge me for the x-ray and seventy-five dollars. (*Pause.*) I'm not going to pay it. (*Pause.*)

Doctor: These are my charges, for an office visit. For the first visit.

Woman: Well, you can find someone who will pay them, then, because I am not going to. (*Pause.*)

Doctor: There is a, there's a *contract* here.

Woman: There is, and what is that?

Doctor: You have taken my services; look, I don't like to talk about this.

Woman: I can see why you don't. Look me in the eye, there is a *contract* here? I have defrauded you of *services*? You charge me forty dollars for an x-ray and seventy-five dollars to tell me that my *toe* is broken, and keep me waiting for three hours. You're goddamned *right* that you don't like to talk about it, 'cause you know that you are *wrong*. You *know* you're wrong.

Doctor: Well, you'll just have to take that question up with my accountants.

Woman: Fine. With your collection agency. Fine. I'll talk to them. I'll see you in small claims court. I don't care. This is not right. You call yourself a doctor. What you are is a thief. *You* live with yourself. No, I'm sorry. Prices what they are, *you* go out and work for a living. *You* go out there and support your family through what you do, and then tell me I should pay that to you. *You* do that. It's *nothing* to you. Nothing, to make people small. To deal with people who are frightened, who are hurt, I don't know, maybe who might think they're dying, and to keep them there *because* they're frightened, and then rob them. Go to hell, you can just go to hell. I damn you. Do you hear me? With your medical car license plates, and tell me there are exigencies? You can go to hell. I'll die before I'll pay that bill. I swear before God. Do you hear me?

Doctor: There's a distinct possibility...

Woman: You kiss my ass!

THE HAT

Customer: What do you think?

Saleswoman: You look wonderful. (*Pause.*)

Customer: Do you think so?

Saleswoman: I do.

Customer: With the veil?

Saleswoman: I don't know. Let's see. Let's try it on.

Customer: With this coat, though.

Saleswoman: Yes. Absolutely. (*Pause.*)

Customer: I'm going out tomorrow on this *interview?*

Saleswoman: Uh-huh.

Customer: No. I don't like the veil. This hat, though, with this coat. (*Saleswoman nods.*) Yes.

Saleswoman: I think that's the nicest coat this season.

Customer: Do you think so?

Saleswoman: Far and away. Far and away.

Customer: Alright. I need the hat. This hat, this coat. (*Pause.*) This bag? (*Pause.*)

Saleswoman: For an interview?

Customer: Yes.

Saleswoman: I'm going to say "no."

Customer: No. I knew you would say that. No. You're right. Alright. The hat, the coat...oh, this is going to cost me, I know...not these boots, though?

Saleswoman: No.

Customer: Too casual.

Saleswoman: Yes.

Customer: Alright. Boots. Something dark. Black.

Saleswoman: ... You have those ankle boots ... ?

Customer: No, no, I want real boots. Dark. Long.

Saleswoman: Severe.

Customer: Very severe ... alright. I need the boots. (*Pause.*) Pants?

Saleswoman: Or a skirt.

Customer: I thought pants. Something in dark green. You know? (*Pause.*)

Saleswoman: Well, you would have to be careful.

Customer: I know, I know. No, I know I would. And I thought a shawl-neck sweater. Something soft.

Saleswoman: Uh-huh.

Customer: In white. (*Pause.*) In off-white. In eggshell.

Saleswoman: Good. Sure.

Customer: This is going to cost me. But I *want* ... do you know?

Saleswoman: Yes.

Customer: I *want*. When I walk *in* there ...

Saleswoman: Yes

Customer: I *want*. (*Pause.*) What do you think? Pants?

Saleswoman: Well, if you feel comfortable ...

Customer: I would, I would. You know why? 'Cause it says something.

Saleswoman: Uh-huh.

Customer: And it holds me in. It makes me stand up. I saw the ones that I want.

Saleswoman: Here?

Customer: Upstairs. Yes. A hundred-twenty dollars. (*Pause.*) What do you think on top?

Saleswoman: You've got the *sweater* ...

Customer: Underneath.

Saleswoman: ... Well ...

Customer: Oh. Oh! You know what? I saw it last month. You know, you know, underthings, an undergarment. (*Pause.*) One piece, you know, like a camisole.

Saleswoman: A teddy.

Customer: Yes. Yes. Just a little lace.

Saleswoman: That would be nice.

Customer: Silk. (*Pause.*) A teddy. Just a little *off*. A little *flush*, what do they call it, beige...

Saleswoman: Uh-huh.

Customer: Not really beige. A little blusher. (*Smiles.*) I put a little blusher underneath. (*Pause.*) Just beneath the lace. Mmm? (*Saleswoman nods.*)

Customer: Alright. The slacks, the teddy, not the bag, the boots, the sweater. (*Pause.*) This is going to cost five hundred dollars.

Saleswoman: No.

Customer: Yes. With a new bag. Yes. (*Pause.*) But it's worth it, right? If I know when I walk in there?

Saleswoman: Yes.

Customer: Look! Look! Oh, look, look what she's got. The clutch bag. Yes. That bag. Yes. Do you think? With this coat.

Saleswoman: Yes.

Customer: 'Cause, 'cause, you know why? You've *got* it. Under *here*. (*Clutches imaginary bag under her arm.*) You know? So when you walk in there... you know? Just...just a small...just...just the perfect...you know? (*Pause.*) I have to have that bag. (*Pause. Shrugs.*) Yes, that bag. The slacks, the teddy, sweater... I couldn't get by with these boots, huh?

Saleswoman: No.

Customer: I know. They're great, though.

Saleswoman: Yes. They are.

Customer (*Sighs*): That bag's got to be two hundred dollars. (*Pause.*) How much is the hat?

Saleswoman: With or without the veil? (*Pause.*)

Customer: Without.

Saleswoman: Fifty-eight dollars.

Customer: And you're sure that you like it.

Saleswoman: You look lovely in it.

Customer: With this coat.

Saleswoman: With that coat. Absolutely.

Customer (*Pause*): I think so. (*Pause.*) I'll take it. Thank you. Thank you. You've been very...

Saleswoman: Not at all.

Customer: No, no. You have. You have been very gracious.

Saleswoman: Not at all.

Customer: Because I want to look nice for tomorrow.

Saleswoman: Well, you will.

Customer (*Nods*): Yes. Thank you. (*To self.*) With this hat.

Saleswoman: Anything else?

Customer: No.

BUSINESSMEN

On an airplane.

Grey: ...Yes yes. We *had* eaten there!

Black: How did you find it?

Grey: Well...

Black: What did you have?

Grey: We had the fish.

Black: We never had the fish.

Grey: It wasn't good. (*Pause.*)

Black: No?

Grey: No. Not at all.

Black: We never had the fish.

Grey: It was not good.

Black: No?

Grey: No. (*Pause.*) It could have been that *night.*

Black: Uh-huh.

Grey: I don't know. (*Pause.*)

Black: Well, we always enjoyed it greatly.

Grey: I'm sure. I am sure. No. (*Pause.*) The atmosphere was *fine.* The *wine*, the *wine* was good...

Black: Uh-huh.

Grey: The *service*...

Black: Uh-huh.

Grey: No. (*Pause.*) No, we should go back again.

Black: You should.

Grey: No. I think that we should.

Black: It probably was that night.

Grey: Yes. (*Pause.*) It very, very well could *have* been. (*Pause.*)

Black: What was it?

Grey: Sole.

Black: Mm. With sauce?

Grey: Yes. With some white wine sauce.

Black: Uh-huh...

Grey: *You* know, with a...*yellow* sauce.

Black: Uh-huh.

Grey: No, I'm sure that it was the fish. (*Nods.*) Fresh fish ...(*Shakes head.*) You never know. (*Pause.*) No. When I was in the army we had one whole company down sick one week.

Black: From fish?

Grey: Uh-huh.

Black: Yes?

Grey: Fish soup.

Black: Uh-huh. I don't doubt it.

Grey: Sick as dogs.

Black: Where was this?

Grey: Fort Sheridan.

Black: Uh-huh.

Grey: Outside Chicago.

Black: Uh-huh. (*Pause.*)

Grey: Sick as dogs. (*Pause.*)

Black: And this was your company?

Grey: No. No, thank God.

Black: Uh-huh. (*Pause.*)

Grey: No. Got out of that one. (*Pause.*)

Black: Mmm. (*Pause.*)

Grey: I missed that one somehow.

Black: Uh-huh.

Grey: I think that that's about the only *one* I missed.

Black: Uh-huh.

Grey: You in the army?

Black: No.

Grey: Armed services?

Black: No. (*Pause.*)

Grey: Uh-huh. Uh-huh. (*Pause.*) Yep. (*Pause.*) Used to go down into *Chicago* weekends.

Black: Uh-huh.

Grey: Raise all *kind* of hell down there.

Black: Down in Chicago.

Grey: Well, yeah. The base is just about an hour bus ride from *town*, eh? Fort *Sheridan*.

Black: Uh-huh.

Grey (*Meditatively*): Yep. (*Pause.*) There used to be this *chili* parlor on the, just across, just kitty-corner from the bus, on, on the *corner*...the *corner* of Clark and Lake Streets. Underneath the Elevated. (*Pause.*)

Black: Uh-huh.

Grey: *Good* chili. (*Pause.*) Good chili. (*Pause.*) Good coffee. (*Pause.*) My *God* that tasted good, out in the cold. (*Pause.*) In those cold winters. (*Pause.*) I can still taste it. We would sit, we would sit in the window, steamy. Smoking *cigarettes*. (*Pause.*) Looking out the window. Underneath the El... (*Pause.*) Steamy...(*Pause.*) Well, I'd better get some *work* done here. (*Takes out pad and pencil.*)

Black: Yes, I best had, too.

Grey: You going home?

Black: No, going to work. (*Pause.*) You?

Grey: Going home.

Black: Good for you.

COLD

A *man,* A, *waiting for a subway; another man,* B, *comes down into the subway and looks up and down the track.*

A: Everybody always looks both ways. Although they always know which way the train is coming from. Did you ever notice that?

B: Yes. I did. (*Pause.*)

A: You going home?

B: Yes. (*Pause.*)

A: I'm going home, too... Did you ever notice sometimes when it's cold you feel *wet*? (*Pause.*)

B: Yes. (*Pause.* A *looks up.*)

A (*Of grating overhead*): They make those things to let in *air.* (*Pause.*)

B: Uh-huh.

A: From outside. Listen: Listen.... (*Pause.*) Where are you going now?

B: Home.

A: Do you live near here?

B: No.

A: Where do you live? (*Pause.*)

B: Downtown.

A: Where?

B: Downtown.

A: Where, though? (*Pause.*)

B: In Soho.

A: Is it nice there?

B: Yes.

A (*Pause*): Is it warm?

B: Yes. (*Pause.*) Sometimes it's not so warm.

A: When wind gets in, right? When the wind gets in?

B: Right.

A: So what do you do then? (*Pause.*) What do you do then?

B: You...stop it up.

A: Uh-huh. (*Pause.*)

B: *Or*...you can put covers on the windows.

A: Covers.

B: Yes. Storm covers. (*Pause.*)

A: Storm covers.

B: To keep out the draft.

A: And does that keep the draft out?

B: Yes.

A: Have you been waiting long?

B: No. (*Pause.*)

A: *How* long? (*Pause.*)

B: Several minutes. (*Pause.*)

A: Are you going home now?

B: Yes. (*Looks at sound of subway in the distance.*)

A: That's the other track. (*They watch the train passing.*) Do you live alone?

B: No. (*Pause.*)

A: You live with someone?

B: Yes.

A: Are you happy? (*Pause.*)

B: Yes.

A: Are they there now?

B (*Pause*): I think so. (*Pause.*)

A: What are they called?

B: Hey, look, what business is it of yours what they're called. (*Pause.*) You understand? (*Pause.*)

EPILOGUE

Man: I love the way the sun goes down. One moment it is dark, the next, light.

A Sermon

A *Sermon* was written as a companion piece for a 1979 Chicago revival of *Sexual Perversity in Chicago*. It featured Cosmo White and, later, W. H. Macy, directed by Sheldon Patinkin.

Character: *Clergyman*

In September, 1939, a dentist in Viceroy, Louisiana, placed a human tooth into a jar of Coca-Cola and let it stand overnight. The next morning Hitler invaded Poland. A man has a deaf yak. The yak cannot hear. It grew up deaf. And this man speaks to it: "How are you today, King?" "Bow wow," says the yak one day. Bow wow. And the next day the yak goes "moo." (*Pause.*) The *an*imal has no *idea* of its responsi*bil*ities. It knows that something is required of it; it knows that it should make a *sound*, but it has no idea what that sound is supposed to be. Life is like that. I feel. If it were not one thing, it would surely be another. It *is*, however, one thing. Though it is by no means the *same* thing. Although it's always something of that nature.

And kindness starts at home. You cannot beat your pets and come quick on your wife and pretend you forgot to take the garbage out and go be nice to whales. It's not *right*, it's trans*par*ent, and it makes you *look* bad, too.

Our most cherished illusions—what are they but hastily constructed cofferdams restraining homosexual panic.

Let's talk about love. (*Pause.*) Love. My golly, it sells diapers, don't it!

Love is the mucilage that sticks the tattered ribbons of experience—the stiff construction-paper Indians and pumpkins of experience—to the scrapbook of our lives.

And there may be many *kinds* of love:

Love may be the Rocky Coast of Maine, with boats and salt spray gooshing up and you all cozy in the rented cabin.

All the others have gone down. Gone down to Boston, gone back to New York. His hands are pressing into the small of your back. His breath is hot upon your shoulder. You have come to write and he has forced the lock. You've never *seen* this man, he followed you home from the pier. But do you care? You care very much. You whack him with the cover of your typewriter. Whack, whack, whack. Whack, whack, whack. Whack, whack, whack. You hit him on the head. And he gets off, he pulls his trousers up and leaves. (*Pause.*) You go back to work. You're typing. "September 18th. Today dawned bleak and sere and I was up to see it. Surely there must be an end to time..."

You look down to read back your sentence to yourself.

What do you see but weak and colorless impressions. Your ribbon has run out. Oh well, that's a fair excuse to go up to the Lodge to share a cup of coffee with the Kind Old Woman who runs the resort.

You open the door. You breathe in the cold, life-giving spray. The Old Man from the Pier hits you on the head with an oar and he jumps on your bones. And this time he has brought his friends.

And what of Death? (*Pause.*) What *of* it? That's my question. All of us are going to die, but nobody believes it. And if we did believe it we would not go to the office. We would call in sick.

Everybody's talking about "Death." Nobody's been there. Yes, yes, yes, there is a rash of testimony to the effect that Ms. So-and-So or Mr. Whossis once was dead for thirty seconds, or something, and it was just like going through a car wash.

You lay back and it is warm and wet outside. But you feel nothing. Whiirrrr, whiirrrr, and here comes the soap. And everything clouds over. Then you hear a hum. And that must be the brushes. Everything goes white, then black, then white again. You feel a buffeting. There is a wall of water/It cascades over the windshield, wetting all, and driving off the sludge, the salt, the road dirt and the soap. Until you're clean. You're clean.

Then comes the hot wax. Analogous in the experience of death to—what? (*Pause.*) *Exactly.* Hot wax coursing for a mere half-dollar more with ten bucks worth of gas. (Well worth it) making your car shine. Shine on. Shine on, my car. (*Pause.*)

Five youths dressed in coveralls drop upon you like ministering angels, rub your imperfections out and then move on. You'd better *tip* them, though, cause you'll be back this way again! There you go. Out into traffic. And how *proud* you feel. And why not? (*Pause.*) This is death. You've been there *before*, you say ... well, you're going there again.

And sickness. Is it real?

And suffering? (*Pause.*) Are they real? (*Pause.*)

Yesterday a man was going to the supermarket. There he went. Upon some errand. His head full of news or gossip.

Fiscal problems...(They are never really far away...) He
turned the corner and he trod upon the mat which would
open the door, and he walked on. The door, however, some
of you have already guessed, did not open. Not a jot. (*Pause.*)
He slammed right into it and broke his nose.

His blood flowed. As many times may happen, attendant
upon a sharper blow to that area—particularly such a blow
to one unused to violent contact—he began to cry. (*Pause.*)

Many who had seen his accident were laughing at the
picture that it made. And then we heard him cry. And then
he turned, and then we saw the blood. (*Pause.*)

"I've broke my nose," he rather oinked. "I've broke my
nose, and you think it's funny." (*Pause.*) He could not think
of what to say; a phrase which might instill in us, the spec-
tators who deigned to ridicule his pain, shame or remorse.
His mind searched for a curse. (*Pause.*) "Fuck you," he said.
(*Pause.*) Fuck you.

What is required of us? To whom do we owe allegiance,
and is this a laughing matter, or should we just mope around
as if the dog died?

This is a good question, and in conclusion, let me say
the following:

A traveler is in the desert. He has lost his way. He has
no water. And he is near death. Far off he sees a mountain.
In the distance. Far away. Ice encapsulates its top and flows
in freshets down its sides, and becomes springs and rivers.
Cool, fresh water, redolent of trout. Clean, unpolluted, there
for all to drink, to bathe in, to enjoy. And he knows it is a
mirage. (*Pause.*) There *is* no mountain there. There is but
desert. But he trudges on toward it in any case. (*Pause.*)
Whom should we identify with in this story? (*Pause.*) How
many thought the trout? It's not the trout. It's not the trout
at all. We've *all* been down. We've all been at the end of
our rope. We all know what it is to call on powers—and
let's pray that they exist—far greater than ourselves; to call
out, "Lord...Lord, this world of yours sucks *hippo* dick, I
just can't hack it anymore." And what answer was forthcom-
ing? (*Pause.*) Exactly.

Therefore, let's smile. Let's slap a silly grin on our face
that says to all the world, "Yes, I see what's going on, but

I'm pretending not to notice. I see the misery...the pain
...the hopes frustrated in our daily lives...the fear of
loneliness...the fear of death..." I'm going to skip to the
end of this list "...and through it all I *smile*, and I say, with
the prophets: 'Lo, this world has been the same a great long
while. It all shall be the same a hundred years from now—
probably sooner.'" (*Pause.*)

　　And that's it.

　　Therefore be well. Peace to you. Be very kind to one
another in your daily lives. And clean up when you're done.

　　Good evening, and Amen.

Shoeshine

Shoeshine was first produced at The Ensemble Studio Theatre in New York with the following cast directed by W. H. Macy: Everett Ensley, Arthur French, Pirie MacDonald, Joseph Jamroy, Colin Stinton, and Trey Hunt.

Scene: *Sam's Shoeshine Parlor. Afternoon.*

Characters
Sam, *a middle-aged black man.*
Jim, *a young black man.*
Miller *and* Fox, *two middle-aged white men.*
Dowd, *a white man.*
Customer, *a white man.*

Jim: You want me to do these?

Sam: They got a shine ticket on it?

Jim: I *saw* it...

Sam: You did...?

Jim: Yeah. It must of gone down in the boot.

Sam: No, no. I'm saying that it *has* a ticket on it.

Jim: I know that it has. I got it. Here it is. (*Pause.*) You want me to do 'em?

Sam: Yeah. You start on 'em.

Jim: Which ones here?

Sam: The *brown* there. Just like you're doing.

Jim: Alright. (*Pause.*)

Sam: And those ones there?

Jim: The red?

Sam: Yeah.

Jim: Uh-huh...

Sam: When you get to them you tell me.

Jim: Alright.

Sam: 'Cause that bitch come in here yesterday...

Jim: Uh-huh.

Sam: She said we fucked them up.

Jim: We didn't fuck them up.

Sam: I know we didn't. (*Pause.*)

Jim: She fucked 'em up her *own* self if she fucked 'em up.

Sam: I know she did. (*Pause.*)

Jim: Uh-huh. (*Pause.*) You got a cigarette? (*Sam takes out his pack of cigarettes. Jim comes over and takes two.*) Thank you.

Sam: That's alright.

Jim: I went down Fifty-seven Street last night.

Sam: Uh-huh. And how was that?

Jim: Yeah. You know. Down on Fifty-eight Street there.

Sam: Uh-huh. You have a good time?

Jim: Yeah.

Sam: Uh-huh.

Jim: Yeah. I was glad to be there.

Sam: I bet that you were.

(Miller *and* Fox *enter.*)

Miller: They make me tired and after a point I can't say I blame them.

Sam: Yessir. You get up there.

Miller (*Referring to Fox*): Me and my man here both.

Fox: No. I don't need a shine.

Miller: Come on, now, let me get you.

Fox: No, I got shined up yesterday.

Sam: We gonna get you now.

(Miller *and* Fox *climb up on the shoeshine stand.*)

Fox (*Waving Sam off*): I'm alright.

Sam (*Starting on Miller*): Yessuh! (*Pause.*)

Jim (*Of shoes*): Sucker dropped these in the *mud*...

(Miller *sighs loudly.*)

Fox: Uh-huh. (*Pause.*)

Miller: The whole thing.

Fox: Yeah.

Sam: You got some salt here.

Miller: Uh-huh. (*Pause.*)

Sam: You want me to take it off?

Miller: What do you use to get it off?

Sam: What? (*Pause.*)

Miller: What do you use to get the salt off?

Jim: ... Down on Fifty-*eight* Street.

Sam: Don't you worry now. We get it off.

Miller (*To* Fox): You got'em shined up yesterday.

Fox: Uh-huh. (*Pause.*)

Miller: Hmmm.

(Fox *picks up a newspaper.*)

Sam: Yessir. You take that paper. That's for you.

Jim: Want me to do these clear ones?

Sam: Yeah. You do them with the saddle soap.

Miller (*To* Fox *of paper*): What's in there?

Fox: Nothing. (*Pause.*)

Miller: You go down to Intercorp?

Fox: No.

Miller: John Reynolds saw you down there.

Fox: Well, I only stopped by.

Miller: Why?

Fox: You know.

Miller: No.

Fox: To talk to some people.

Miller: Uh-huh. Yeah. I wouldn't take it, you know.

Fox: No?

Miller: Uh-huh. They offered it to me.

Fox: I wish they'd offered it to me.

Miller: You'd be a fool to talk to them. I think you'd be a fool to go in there.

Fox: Come on, I only went down to say hello.

Jim: ... The *saddle* soap.

Miller: And how is everyone down there?

Fox: Fine.

(Dowd *enters.*)

Sam (*To* Dowd): Yessuh. Did you forget something?

Dowd: I think I lost my wallet here.

Miller: I saw where Charlie Beeman's moved.

Fox: Where were you sitting?

Dowd: Up there.

(Miller *and* Fox *search for the wallet. Pause.*)

Fox: It isn't here.

Miller: How long ago'd you...

Dowd: Just a minute...

Sam: Just before you came.

Miller: Huh! (*Pause.*)

Dowd: None of you saw a wallet here?

Miller: No.

Sam: Jimmy...?

Fox: No.

Jim: What?

Sam: You seen a wallet?

Jim: No. (*Pause.*)

Sam: I'm sorry, mister.

Jim:...What? I seen a *wallet*?

Sam: Yeah.

Jim: No. (*Pause.*)

Sam: I'm sorry, mister. (*Pause.*) You can look around. Ain't no one moved since you left.

Dowd: Could I talk to you? (*Starts taking Sam aside.*)

Sam: Uh?

Dowd: Please, one moment. (*Takes him aside.*)

Miller: Uh, buddy, can your friend finish me up?

Sam: Jim, you finish up that man. (*Jim goes to do so.*)

Dowd: Now, I had a lot of   **Miller:** I knew him back at

money, I just cashed a check, and...

Sam: Mister, I swear on my life...

Dowd: No, wait a second.

C & D, you know?

Fox: Yeah?

Miller: Oh *yeah*. Son of a bitch then...

Fox: Uh-huh.

Jim: You using the saddle soap on these?

Sam: Yes. I am.

Jim: Alright.

Miller: You'll finish off the bottoms with the brown...?

Jim: Sure will.

Dowd: Listen to me; I'd hate to have to *do* anything about this.

Sam: Do what you want, we didn't find your billfold here.

Dowd: It's not the money, do you understand?

Miller: I mean, you want to spend your time in office politics you're going to rise.

Fox: Uh-huh.

Miller: You want to *do* it that way.

Fox: Yeah.

Sam: I understand it all. I just can't help you.

Dowd: I would hate to have to go and get the cops.

Sam: Mister, you trace your steps back. *I* don't know...

Miller: Where were you before you were here?

Dowd: Next door.

Miller (*To* Fox): ...You want to brown-nose your way through *life*...

Dowd (*To Sam*): Look, look, I'll give you one-third of the money if I get the wallet back. (*Pause.*) With all the cards.

Miller: ...If you're content to live your life like that. I told him one day, "I'm a maverick, Charl, I can't live life your way. I got to go out there. You don't have to go in the houses."

Jim: How much was in it?   **Fox:** Yeah.

Dowd: Did you take it?   **Miller:** *Huh*?

Jim: No.

Dowd: Then what the fuck business do you have asking how much was in it?

Sam: You go an' call your cops.

Miller: I mean if you want to get *Byzantine* ...

Jim: I was just asking, sucker.

Dowd: You've got no business to know.

Jim: I don't?

Dowd: You absolutely don't.

Jim: Unless I took it.

Dowd: Uh-huh, yeah.

Jim: An' then I *know* how much it was.

Dowd: That's right.

Jim: So what the fuck I'm *asking* for? You motherfucker, get out of this store.

Dowd: I don't want to come back here with the police ...

Sam: You come back however you want. Now we don't have your money. If we had it, we would give it to you. (*Pause. Dowd exits.*) Oooeee! Now there's a fellow that was *mad* ...

Jim: ... Sonofabitch ...

Sam: That sucker's *mad* ...   **Miller:** I mean, if you want to brown-nose your way through life. It isn't worth it. Fuck it.

Jim: ... Come in here like the   **Fox:** Yeah.
viceroy of some place.

Sam: Sucker come in here yesterday ...

Jim: Yeah ...

Sam: Me an Bill here, he say, "Which one of you fellows

going to give me a fine *shine* today?"

Miller: You're going to do that brown thing?

Jim: Yeah. I'll do her.

Miller: In fifty years who's going to know who went to Maui with the boss.

Sam: "Which one o' you fellows going to give me a *shoeshine* today!"

Jim: Hnuh!

Miller: ...They wonder why the people walk.

Fox: Uh-huh.

Sam: "Get up," Bill say, "You want your shoes shined you get up there."

Miller: ...Not one word of backing.

Fox: No.

Jim: He get up?

Sam: Yeah. He got up there.

Miller: I'm sorry...

Jim: ...Sonofabitch.

Miller: ...Buddy up to you at Christmas if you made the list...

Sam: "Which one you mens goan shine my nice sweet shoes today..."

Miller: He wants his picture with his arm around you in the Trades...

Jim: ...Sonofabitch.

Miller: And if you didn't make the list that year, fuck you.

Fox: Uh-huh.

Miller: I'm glad that sucker's gone.

Jim (*Of nothing in particular*): Yes*suh*...

Miller: I'll live without him very well.

Sam: How late you stayin' in?

Jim: How late you need me?

Sam: Can you stay 'til six?

Miller: How is he looking?

Fox: Fine.

Jim: You need me?

Sam: Yeah.

Jim: Alright.

Miller: I'll bet he is.

Jim: You done.

Miller (*Rising*): What do I owe you?

Jim: Dollar.

Miller: ... Gone to fucking *Maui* every goddamn month... how much?

Jim: One dollar. (*Pause.*)

Miller: A dollar for a shine?

Jim: Yessuh! (*Pause.*) Thass a *spit* shine!

(*Pause. Miller digs in his pocket and starts to pay.*)

Miller (*To* Sam): Did you find that guy's wallet?

Sam: Shit. No sir. You have a good day now.

Miller (*Exiting, to* Fox): Yeah. I heard you went down there...

Sam: How much he give you?

Jim: Twenny cent.

Sam: Sonofabitch...

(*Pause. Jim goes back to work on uninhabited shoes.*)

Jim: Yeah. They was down on Fifty-seven Street down there.

Sam: Who?

Jim: *You* know. Richard... everybody...

Sam: Uh-huh.

Jim: This stuff don't come off.

Sam: You use some Brillo on it?

Jim: That won't help.

Sam: No?

Jim: Uh-uh. (*Pause.*)

Sam: You try it.

Jim: I will.

Sam: Did you find that fellow's billfold?

Jim: Shit.

Sam: Well did you?

(Customer *enters.*)

Customer: Shoeshine.

Sam: You get up there! (Customer *takes seat, picks up paper.*) Yessuh. Thass right. Thass for you! (*Starts on shoes. To* Jim.) 'Cause if you found that thing you best had tell me.

Jim: No, I didn't find nothin'.

Customer: What did you lose?

Sam: He lost his wallet somewhere in here.

Customer (*Producing cigarette*): Do you have a match?

Sam: Yessuh, I surely do. (*Lights* Customer'*s cigarette. Pause. To* Jim.) 'Cause you know if I found it I'd tell you.

Jim: I know you would.

Sam: You know I would.

Customer: I got a spot of paint or something on the toe.

Sam: Yessuh, I see it.

Jim: ... Yeah, they was all down there drinkin' ...

Sam: Uh-huh. If them people come back here, you best tell the truth.

Jim: I tole the truth.

Sam: Uh-huh.

Jim: I tole the truth.

Sam: We gonna see.

Jim: Well man I tole you what the truth was, so you just think what you want.

Sam: I will.

Jim: How late you say you want me to stay today?

Sam: Thass up to you—I'm stayin' to six.

Jim: I'll stay too.

Sam: Yeah, you do what you want.

Jim: Shit.

Sam: Fine pair of shoes you got here.

Customer: Thank you.

Jim: I'm gettin' to the red.

Sam: You call me 'fore you do 'em.

Jim: Yes I will. (*To self.*)...She said we fucked 'em up...

Sam: Huh?

Jim: Yeah. I'm glad I wasn't here.

Sam: Well, don't you worry. She be back.

Jim: Uh-huh. (*Pause.*) How I know *you* didn't find it.

Sam: Shit, I found it man, how come I'm askin' you?

Jim: Uh-huh.

Litko: A Dramatic Monologue

Litko: A Dramatic Monologue was written as a companion piece for *The Duck Variations* in its 1973 Chicago premiere at the Body Politic, and featured Jim Brett directed by David Mamet.

Character: *Litko*

Litko: (At rise Litko is discovered addressing the audience. Litko speaks.) Do we understand each other?

His demeanor and, in fact, his line ("Do we understand each other?") go far in helping to create a bond between Litko and his audience. Unbutton coat. Litko speaks: Let us dispense with formality, and get down to theatrical cliches.

The audience smiles appreciatively at his candid behavior.

Thanks, gang. Pause.

"I wonder if they realize the technical proficiency and purely traditional dramatic training necessary to establish the actor's comfort in a setting ostensibly devoid of qualities." Paper, mister?

"You can't go out there, Litko," he says to the audience. "Billy Brenneer and the *Lazy 'J'* boys'll cut you down like a muskrat." Many members of the audience wonder if they really know what a muskrat is. Litko assures them it is not important. "It is not important." That's easy for him to say.

A pause (or silence) ensues, broken only by sporadic coughing and the line "broken only by sporadic coughing and the line."

It becomes obvious to both parties to the theatrical *event*, that a crux has been reached. Progression of some sort is clearly indicated.

A new character seems unlikely.

Introduction of further vocabulary is certainly within the limits of accepted tradition.

The appearance of a goofy prop or two ... (don't hold your breath).

The re-occurrence of World War One ... ?

Police brutality?

The news that some wild animal has escaped from a nearby zoo, and is believed hiding *right here in this theater*! (I'm spelling that "E," "R.") (At this point I shall go and look—or pretend to look—you're grownups, judge for yourselves—at several places around the stage where this alleged animal might hide.) (But Litko does not move.) Which might just raise a question as to the responsibility of the dramatic artist to his audience. (What sophistry!) I will now deliver myself of the following: one of a number of previously prepared and memorized speeches:

"I love you. I have always loved you. I shall love you as long as there courses in my veins—and, to be realistic, in *your* veins—blood." Let us recapitulate. (Why? because it *feels* so good.) A while ago a person unknown to you...

"Of course," Litko allows, "some of you," addressing the audience directly—what high style!—"do know this person," indicating himself, "in another guise, or in different guises. But," he says, "I sincerely hope," leaving for the audience to decide for itself or themselves the veracity of the aforementioned hope, and whether the said hope is that of the character (that is to say, the *playwright*) or of the actor; and, if *of* the actor, of him truly, or but under the somewhat—let us face the facts—extenuating circumstances in which we now find him, and, just a bit further, if we really got the time for this diversion...

"I sincerely hope..." or, from another tack:

"In response to a tacit yet undeniable inquiry into the sincerity of my hope..." and

"As to the current employment of that which, believe me, can be taken as my true capacity for sincerity..." let us leave no stone unturned, though: "For those who desire the identity of him the sincerity of whose hope has, of late, so clearly manifest itself, let me reply." (No one indicates a reluctance to let him reply.)

Litko confronts his audience: "Hi, gang."

Some, apparently, would appreciate a reply. Or do not care. Or are asleep.

Is a show of hands indicated? (In certain circumstances, yes.)

Why, then, does Litko not reply?

Has he been "struck dumb"?

Shall he lapse into song? Or dance? Or mixed-media? Or some more purely visual form of art? Has he the training? Has he the inclination? Has he the time? Is God dead? (No, I know, that's nothing to joke about.) This is no life for a grown man, Litko says, on the verge of great frenzy. (Emotion is freeing to look at, but tiresome to indulge in.) "A funny thing happened to me," Litko says, humor dripping from each word and gesture.

"Really now, seriously, folks, I have the sorry task of informing you that—yes, you guessed it—the theater is dead" (Oh no.)

"—innocence, your eight-year-old foster child, Scooter, along with a busload of his classmates enroute to the zoo, Beethoven, LaFollette, and countless other individuals and institutions of varying worth." (All of this, of course, having taken place over a period of years, and astonishing only in the aggregate.)

"What can we salvage of this carnage?" Litko asks, imaginary tears coursing down his all-too-real cheeks, "Hope for the future? The odd wristwatch?"

(Wait a second, please.)

"How old are you, Trigger?"

(While my imaginary horse is counting, folks, and in the final seconds of our time together here I'd like to say, on behalf of myself, the author, the director, our wonderful stagehands—seriously, don't they do a great job?—our house crew, *their* families, and the many, many men and women who provide them with the services and goods so necessary for the support of life: keep your pecker up.)

Anybody out there from Kankakee!?

In Old Vermont

Characters: *Roger, Maud*

Roger: Do you remember when we were in Vermont that time?

Maud: Of course.

Roger: Do you remember that?

Maud: Yes. (*Pause.*) The sky.

Roger: The sky. Yes.

Maud: Cold. The cold. The evenings. Sitting.

Roger: "Old, old, old New England."

Maud: Fire.

Roger: The fire. Oh, yes.

Maud: I like the mornings. Do you know why?

Roger: Why?

Maud: It will become warm.

Also, in the evenings. When the sun goes down. In afternoons.

In winter. When the sun goes down.

It becomes warm. In afternoon. The sun shines.

All the snow is bright.

The cold protects us.

It can warm us.

In the winter.

In the snow.

Like skating on the ice.

The shock comes.

With the fissure. Falling. (*Pause.*)

For moments.

For one moment. When you know that you are cold. (*Pause.*)

Then it seeps in.

When the cold comes it is warm.

As if you'd wet the bed.

The rabbits turn. They turn to white.

I like it in the winter. For we ... For we are *protected.* (*Pause.*)

You hear?

THEN WE ARE ALONE!

IN A VACATION HOME. WE'RE WAITING!
FOR THE *WHAT*? THE SPIRIT.

Indians could come. Where would we hide? Where would we go then? We'd not made provisions. It is much too late.

We could have cut a cellar in the ground or made a secret room between the logs, or in the roof.

A deep, deep cellar down. Beneath the rug. *They'd* never find it!

Do not tell me that. Not if you tamped it down. Not if you tamped the dirt down. *Trampled* it and fit the logs in. Covered with an Oriental rug in red.

They'd stomp, they'd stomp, they'd all try to search out our hiding place.

But they could not. They couldn't *find* it.

So don't tell me that.

If we had built it. If we'd built it. If we'd took the time. But no!

The shock of when they come.

The tommyhawk.

The genitals hacked off.

The cold and roasting flesh.

Your own hands severed and your eyes like boils.

Like fevered boils, like ponds. Like flying geese.

Our screams mean nothing.

Far above the summer scene.

The hot. The sickly heat.

The fire. Burning down.

The wings.

The flapping of the windowshade.

The upturned lamp.

A candle guttered.

Someone finds a bag of salt.

That they had overturned.

(*A long pause.*)

In old Vermont.

All Men Are Whores: An Inquiry

All Men Are Whores was first presented in February, 1977 at the Yale Cabaret with the following cast directed by David Mamet: Patti LuPone, Kevin Kline, and Sam Tsoutsovas.

Characters: *Sam, Kevin, Patti*

One

Sam: Our concept of time is predicated upon our understanding of death.

Time passes solely because death ends time. Our understanding of death is arrived at, in the main, because of the nature of sexual reproduction.

Organisms which reproduce through fission do not "die."

The stream of life, the continuation of the germ plasm, is unbroken.

Clearly.

Just as it is in the case of man.

But much less apparently so in our case. For we are sentient.

We are conscious of ourselves, and conscious of the schism in our sexuality.

And so we perceive time. (*Pause.*) And so we will do anything for some affection.

Two

Kevin: I saw her in the Art Institute four years ago. I saw her from the back, her neck, she sat up. Near the Oriental art. The horses. She faced down away from me her hair was dark, she had a cotton suit on.

I looked at her a long time at her back. I thought that if you walk away from her you'll always wish you had (I knew that I would think about her).

In the way she faced away from me I couldn't see her.

I went over to the case in front of her. (*Pause.*)

She had been out in the sun.

Hello. She looked at me. I stood there. I saw that she was reading she had put her book aside.

A long time. (*Pause.*)

She put her hand on my arm she smelled, I don't know,

like musk, faint brushing hair on her neck, back, wisps...

Slowly, in the cloakroom, in the hall I said that I just live a little way from here.

She put her head down on my shoulder in the taxicab, I wondered how can someone be so light, she took my chin and kissed me, she put my hand underneath her dress and rubbed my hand against her.

I just live on the second floor, she nodded, we went up.

I took her jacket, take me in the bedroom, she said.

She was like an otter, she was sleek. (*Pause.*)

I'm glad we met, I said, you make me feel good.

What, was I asleep, she said? (*Pause.*)

Please. What time is it?

I helped her find her things I took her face to kiss her.

Please, I have to go, she told me.

Are You married, I said, no. Oh. Will you call me?

Yes.

You have the number?

Are you in the book, she said? (*Pause.*)

Yes.

Good...(*Pause.*)

When I saw her on the bus a month ago, Hello, I said. I'll bet that you don't remember me. (*Pause.*)

Have you been here this whole time? (*Pause.*) Have you been here all this time?

Three

Sam: If we could reproduce like paramecia do you think that we would not?

When the secrets of the age were clear to him he took it like a man, which is to say as one who has no choice.

Four

Patti: He said he thought of me with great affection, still. He had this fantasy where he came over and he knew something was wrong, he came in I was in the kitchen here there was this huge, ah, I don't know, a maniac, he'd hurt me, he had hurt my face, he bruised me, I had bruises on my breasts, I had become all helpless, I thought I was going to die and I was whimpering when he came in he saw what the man was doing, and he filled with rage, he tore him off of me and threw him on the floor and killed him.

He says, "You should not be let to live," he did vile things to him, I don't know, he kicked him in the testicles, or put his eyes out. (*Pause.*)

Because he'd hurt me and this filled him with such rage the man should not be let to live. Because he thought of me with great affection still.

Five

Kevin: Oh. (*Pause.*) Those cool forearms on my shoulder.

Her blue shirt was tied around her waist.

I licked her armpits.

Sweat. Her shirt. She kept her shirt on, I unbuttoned it and kissed her breasts. (Our bellies got so slippery.)

That morning, when she woke up, at the sink, her pants, her cotton pants, she washed her hair out at the sink, and when she took her shirt off I came up behind and held onto her breasts and she told me to wait, she would be done, wait, when she got the soap off.

We sat on the porch. (*Pause.*) Please make love to me.

Please tell me that you'd like for me to do things to you.

In my dream I dreamt you would. (*Pause.*) I always dreamt you would. I knew you would.

Six

Sam: I like a nice ass.

I like a nice ass and legs. (*Pause.*)

The ass is the top of the legs.

Seven

Patti: He said that what he thought that beauty was, that *beauty* was the striving, the unconscious striving of the germ plasm to find a mate who would, when coupled with itself, improve the race. (*Pause.*)

He thought that those things we found beautiful were those which would improve the race. (Is that right? Yes. Alright.)

So, What, I said, big titties and firm thighs and things for bearing in the fields? Right? He told me no. That we were overpopulated and we now need something else.

And those things which we need form our ideas of what's beautiful.

Oh. Yes, I said, I see: conditioning. Ideas someone places in your mind. Like advertising. No, he said. You cannot step outside the culture: Those who educate you, someone taught them, too.

You see?

I did not see, no, but this turned me on. Please kiss me, I said.

They were educated, too, he said. (No, wait.)

(Alright.)

We strive . . . we strive . . .

To *what*, I said?

We strive . . . our loins . . . we're driven . . . (As a race, I said, or individuals?)

A race.

(A woman of my age would never ask a man to her

apartment for an after-dinner drink unless she wanted him. He surely knows this.)

Wait, do you like Tolstoy, he said?

No. I do not like Tolstoy.

No? Why?

Oh. (*Sighs.*) I don't know.

Many reasons—(*Pause.*)

We find those things beautiful, he said, we feel may improve us.

(Our unconscious longings.)

(I was wet, but now I'm not.)

Yes. Do you read a lot, he asked me?

Yes. I read.

Oh, really, what?

Things. Books.

A long pause came here. You have lovely eyes he said. (*Pause.*) Thank you.

Yes. He said. I like your breasts. Thank you, I said, they're rather small.

I like that, he said. Do you? Yes.

I ran my right hand through his hair.

He sat there for a moment then moved by me on the couch.

Uh...*listen*, he said...

Yes?

Eight

Kevin: I hate your family.

You know, I think there *are* no interesting restaurants.

She would suck me off in taxicabs. (I feel she would.)

I think a man could lose his life with her.

Offstage Voice: Our small cabals.

Kevin: I think her fingers taste of gun oil.

Offstage Voice: Jive mesmery of musk and fish...

Kevin: I think she smells like musk and cordite. We should be down in the West Side by the docks with Browning automatics.

She's a cannibal and who the fuck knows *what* she does. (*Pause.*)

Who have *you* killed?

Eh? When they drop the atom bomb, are you going to make me *soup*????

I want to see tattoos, and fuck you with your eyeshadow. I mean it.

Offstage Voice: Harlotry and necromancy. (*Pause.*)

Kevin: I mean it.

Nine

Patti: I want to tie you to the bed, he said.

Okay, I said.

I want to lick all over you he said, I told him yes, I'd like that.

Would you. Yes. I said.

I want to chain you face down and to bite you all around your pussy.

Okay, I told him. Don't hurt me, though.

He said he wouldn't, but he asked me could he be a little rough. ʼ

I told him sure, just if he didn't hurt me.

He told me that he might just have to be a little rough.

Don't be too rough, I asked him, and he said he'd try not to, but sometimes he thought that it was a good idea for someone to be rough.

Alright, I said, just so long as they are gentle, too. It doesn't matter what you called it just so long as you don't hurt another person.

No, he said, but sometimes just a little pain could be erotic.

Did I think so?

I told him what? What do you mean? You tell me what you want to do, whatever, it's okay or not, but we can talk about it.

I want you to feel good and I want to feel good, too, I want to get out, too, to get off.

You know that I like you.

I told you I like you.

Take your clothes off, he said. Okay, I said.

Now, he told me. Okay, I said, you take yours off, too.

No, he said, I only want to watch, okay.

He told me that he thought I had a lovely body, which was nice.

I told him he should take his clothes off and he said, alright, he would in a minute.

It's alright, I told him. It's alright.

I want to hit you, he said. No, you don't, I said.

I *do*, though, he said.

No, you don't, I said. You know you don't.

I *do*, though, he said.

No, you don't. Come here. Come here. And then I, him, we went, over to the couch and sat down there and I held him a while, we sat there, and I got the blanket later on and put it over us and fell asleep.

Ten

Sam: At the Art Institute. The French Impressionists.

Some salesman from Ohio.

I said, Hello, do you like Mary Cassatt?

He said he thought so, was this one of hers.

I looked. Yes.

He sat. We talked.

He comes in every two weeks. For some company.

I smiled. Let's take a walk.

Oh, he said, sure, if you don't mind. I'd like to see the North Side.

We walked by the lake, down by the Yacht Club (he'd been in the navy).

Such a fine day...

We went back to my...he said Oh, do you *live* around here...? my apartment and we drank a bit.

He told me that the kind (that he was looking) that the sort of a relationship that he was looking for would take a long, long time to, I don't know, to ferment. He said that he thought that people shouldn't go to bed together for some (a certain) measured time, a month, three months...in which to get to know each other well.

He told me that he wanted to be friends with me. He felt we could be close. (These things take time.) Eleven-thirty.

I said, my friend, look: you think (you may think...) you want some lasting...*I* don't know...some lasting something. (Nothing lasts forever...) (I don't know what it is that you want.) But now, tonight, for my *own* self, what I want is to get laid. Thank you. Call me.

Then I took a shower and went out.

Eleven

Kevin: It seemed I had discovered a capacity for being happy with a woman.

When my possession of this talent had occurred to me I rejoiced that I would not be lonely anymore, but move from one affair to yet another learning from each woman with whom I spent time, and living through the periods of my romantic re-alignments with both grace and happy resignation.

Lately, though, I find I am confused. I realize, I think, that one can only learn from these encounters if one makes some sort of compact with the person with whom one is spending time. (*Pause.*)

These contracts, these avowals of desire, of (let us face the facts) *compulsion.* (*Pause.*) They may *increase* desire (or our capacity for such) but limit our ability to act with our newfound and *pro*found emotional resources. (*Pause.*)

How can•this end, other than in great resentment of one's current partner? (*Pause.*)

Quite frankly, how?

Twelve

Patti: We built our fires on the beach, and every night we sat by them and talked and ate our food, and we made love and slept.

As fall came we moved back into the dunes. (*Pause.*)

Later, we went further. To the woods; but walked or fished or searched for clams or driftwood in the mornings and the afternoons. And as we walked we saw the charred-out fires we had built, each in a different place, and said "do you remember that night?" (*Pause.*)

"The night we had that fire? What we ate, and how we touched each other? (*Pause.*) Do you remember?"

Or later, walking in the dunes I'd come across a hill into a gully when the sand had blown—the place was changed, of course, but something still remained. The logs, the angles they had fallen in... It wouldn't be the same when spring came. Traces of our camp would be obliterated by the winter and the shore itself would change. (We thought as we lived back in the trees.) (*Pause.*)

Where we moved back. (*Pause.*)

Where we retired. (*Pause.*)

"Do you remember that night?" we would say...

Thirteen

Sam: Where were you? You weren't there. You know what it means to me when you're late. There's going to come a time when this is life and death, these assignations.

You never fulfill my instructions. You don't.

Do you think that I *care*?

Do you know what I care about? *Loyalty.*

Do you think that I care for six *minutes*?

Eh? What do you think I *am*? Don't you *see*...?

There's going to come a time when this is life and *death*.

There are things going on, there are things going on in this country you cannot be imprecise. You can*not*...! (*Pause.*)

And it just takes you ages to leave anywhere. (And you can't keep your fucking mouth shut.) Do you think that I care for *appearances*? What I care for (What I care for miss) (yes) is *survival. Survival.*

(You're so secure...)

What do you know? You don't know what life is. You know *nothing.*

Fourteen

Kevin: He brought the coffee, it was very good. I lit a cigarette, I looked at her. She smiled.

I have something for you, she said.

Oh, what?

A thing...something. She took a package from her purse, she gave it to me. She smiled.

Shall I open it? Yes, open it.

She's bought me a gold lighter. (*Pause.*)

It's lovely, I said. (*Pause.*) You shouldn't have.

She'd had it engraved with my name. And then "I love you," and her name. It's lovely, I said.

Do you like it?

Yes, I said, you shouldn't have.

She smiled. (*Pause.*) You don't like it.

No, I like it very much, it's lovely.

No. You don't.

I do.

No.

Yes, I do, I told her. (*Pause.*) You shouldn't have though.
No? (*Pause.*) Why? (*Pause.*) Why? (*Pause.*)
Look, I told her. We are friends (are we friends?).
What do you mean "friends"? What?
We are friends, I want to be your friend, I said. (*Pause.*)
What does this mean, she asked me.
Please, not now, I said.
No. Now. Now, please, what does this mean? (*Pause.*)
Look, I told her.
No, she said. Don't tell me this. (*Pause.*) No, don't do
this.
Keep your voice down.
I don't care. (*Pause.*) *I* don't care...
He came back and he stopped and asked if we'd like
some more coffee...
No, she said, don't tell me this. (*Pause.*) No. She started
crying.
Are you alright, I said? What? (*Pause.*) No. Would you
like something? Something? *What?* I don't know, can I get
you something? (Do we have to do this here?) (*Pause.*) Would
you like to leave? (*Pause.*) Shall we leave?
Leave me alone. She got up, he came over to pull out
her chair but she was gone. I sat there. (*Pause.*)
He asked me if I'd care for something else. (*Pause.*)
Some more coffee...(*Pause.*) What? No. (*Pause.*) Yes.
"I love you." (*Pause.*) I lit a cigarette.

Fifteen

Patti: Come here come here.
I know what you want.
You don't have to say it.
I know.
You don't have to say you want it.
I know.
I know; you don't want it. I know.
But come here.

It's alright.
I'm here.
Come on.
No.
Come on.
Yes.
Come here.
You lie down, now.
That's alright.
You lie down.
Good.
That's good.
Good.
Now be quiet. You be quiet now.
I know.
Now I am going to make you feel good.
I know.
You be quiet, now. That's alright.
I know what you want. (*Pause.*)
You don't have to tell me that you want it.
That's alright.
You just be still now.
That's alright. (*Pause.*)
Good.

Sixteen

Sam: The problems of the universe. We are programmed to love our loved ones, all our paramours, our wives, our husbands. (*Pause.*) We are programmed to love our race. To help our race survive.

This is a chemic fiat, and what does it have, I ask you, what, to do with metaphysics? Neither *are* there metaphysics, no. But only more increasingly occult degrees of understanding—hidden, though, only because of our interminable arrogance—Our race-conceit. (Is it true?) We are the stuff that rocks are made of and cannot be broken of the

habit of an intuition of some specialness—(*Pause.*)
    We are the fish.
    When it all comes to chemicals.
    Where are our mothers, now? Where are they? In the moment of our death, or birth, of orgasm or hunger?
    When it all comes down to carbon, or to hydrogen?
    In cities where we kill for comfort—for a moment of reprieve from our adulterated lives—for fellow-feeling. (*Pause.*) (I have eyelashes, too...)
    Some night when you have been up half the night alone when you have read instructions on the phonebook, eh?
    Then, when the walls scream. Eh?
    Who'd sell our soul just to be ratified, in taxicabs, in some resort, along the cradle, by a touch (a friend, our mother...) who would make the world go. (*Pause.*)
    One moment of release.
    Psychic reprieve.
    (Oh, God, what are we doing here?)
    We are uprooted.
    We have no connection. (*Pause.*)
    We beat each other by the docks or dressed in jackboots and in uniforms, and preen in passing windows just like everyone.
    Our life is garbage.
    We take comfort in our work and cruelty. We love the manicurist and the nurse for they hold hands with us. Where is our mother now? We woo with condoms and a ferry ride; the world around us crumples into chemicals, we stand intractable, and wait for someone competent to take us 'cross the street. (*Pause.*)
    Where are our preceptors now? Or at the moment of death, and would *you* not do all you can, forsaking anything, for one swift moment of surcease? (The battered bodies, news photographers, pulp analyses, (*Pause.*) crimson sheets...)
    My god, we've done what we should not have. (*Pause.*)
    I'm sure we must have.

Seventeen

Patti: We wait for someone—

Kevin: Tie me up and beat me.

Patti: Look, I told him, look, what do I care if I am right for you or not (for me or not) (if you are...?)

All I only care is do I want to be with you (because I want to be with you) and that you would make me happy.

Kevin: Yes, I swear to God that if I have to spend another Sunday evening by myself that I am going to blow my brains out.

Patti: Look:

Kevin: Now is this so unreasonable?

Sam: Precious anomalies of lovers' flesh, quirks of behavior, heartbreaking inside curves of thigh. (*Pause.*) The curriculum of small cabals that we endeavor to create or to prolong...

Patti: (Don't stop...)

Sam: ...The search for an exclusive union redolent of salt-water and gun oil; alcohol on cotton balls after tattooing, soap, and liquid-paper...

Kevin: Individuating qualities.

Like fires burnt out on the beach.

Sam: (The orthographical misjudgments in her love letters...)

Patti (*Pause*): Yes.

Sam: Our small cabals. (*Pause.*) And why not?

Kevin: Secret moon-borne signals are denied us, and we spill our seed upon the ground. (*Pause.*)

At the moment of our death we still embrace catholicism or the flag or reach for our executors. (*Pause.*)

Our great epiphany by some bizarre concidence comes at the moment of our death.

Sam: When they get deep. (*Pause.*) Women, when they moan, they go nuts and their voices get deep. They are saying "look (I think) this is not what you think it is," they're saying "look." (*Pause.*)

Kevin: So enthrall to that saline flesh.

Sam: (Yes.)

Patti: We know the organism is by no means perfect. We can admit the possibility of some divine control (or absence of control). Of some Much Greater plan, or oversight. We recognize this in the body, we can see the flesh is far from perfect. We are the repositories of disease and physical disaster. This is patent, and we see that something is mistaken. (*Pause.*) What if this undignified and headlong thrusting toward each other's sex is nothing but an oversight or physical malformity? (*Pause.*)

Should we not, perhaps, retrain ourselves to revel in the sexual act not as the consummation of predestined and regenerate desire, but rather as a two-part affirmation of our need for solace in extremis.

Kevin: (Goodnight.)

Patti: In a world where nothing works.

Sam: No.

Patti: In which we render extreme unction with our genitalia. (*Pause.*)